Lola's Journey

Lola's Journey

Lola Hewitt

Cold Front Publishing

Contents

To my family and those who have crossed my
path and made a difference along the way.

"Lola's Journey with her Angel."

An introduction.

I have felt there was a purpose for me since I was a teenager. I have no idea what it is yet. But just maybe, I am supposed to share my life's journey as an inspiration to help others that may sometimes lose their way in life. We all have a journey in life. Some just have more curves, roadblocks, and events than others. I believe we discover many important things on this journey. Two that I consider to be relevant to who we are would be Memories and Character.

Memories are all about, what you do with them, and how you use them to help or teach others. I am not sure what I would do without my memories. They are all I have left of most of my family. Everyone has a memory that can help another person not make a mistake, feel better about who they are, teach them a life lesson, inspire them, or just make them laugh. No matter what they do, you are both a winner if you share them. Most of your memories need to be shared. They are your life lessons and should be used to teach.

Over the years, I have shared so many memories, and I have heard many times, "You need to write a book." I was told this in April of 2011 by my friend Lori from work, just before I resigned from a company I had been with for over thirty-two years. That was not the reason I resigned. But now I have no reason not to write this book.

So, as I have been told to do so many times, I am going to tell my story as seen through my eyes. I lost my mother when I thought I needed her most, and I was angry at the world *and God* for a very short time. As time passed, I realized that my memories of her made me happy so much more than they made me sad. I realized I had something with her that many women never get. And of her seven children, I was the only one that did get this relationship with her.

The last couple years of her life, she was my mother and my best friend. She trusted me, and I trusted her. I could tell her anything, and she would give me her thoughts and advice. But the last few years, I felt that no matter what, she trusted that I would make good decisions, and she respected me as a woman. It was good. It is something I will cherish forever. Unfortunately, my siblings did not get this relationship with her. They were young during the toughest years of my family's lives. I was much younger.

When my mother passed away, she had been sick for about three years, and we spent a lot of time together. During this time, we really did get to know one another. I would spend the night at her house, and we would stay up talking and laughing for hours and hours, long after everyone went to bed. We would laugh till we were in tears and our sides hurt. And occasionally, we would cry. My life had a lot of sadness in it as a child. And that is mostly what I remembered. But during this time, she helped me find some of the good memories of my childhood that I had tucked away somewhere safe. You see, I believe we too often let our bad memories outweigh the good ones and leave the biggest mark on our lives. The good ones are there. But you store them somewhere safe in your mind and heart so no one can touch them.

Mom told me many times that she was sick, walked with a walker, and was blind at such an early age because she was being punished. God was punishing her. I am not sure that is something God would do. I am sure there were many things I did not know about her life because she truly believed He was. If He was, she did receive more than enough suffering.

My mother was my best friend when she died at fifty-nine years of age. I was twenty-nine. I am so glad we had those last couple years. Even though she was sick, they were very good years for her and me to bond and for her to help me remember old memories and leave me with new ones. If she had not been sick and needed me, I may have never gotten those memories. Sometimes the most awful of times can leave us with memories that will help us get through life. Thanks, Mom.

Most of us figure out eventually that the greatest things in life have no value in dollars whatsoever. Some of us at a much earlier age than others. Having lost my parents, grandparents, one nephew, and a brother before I was twenty-nine was enough to make me start to evaluate the important things in life. I was also going through the end of a marriage at this age. So, turning thirty was the toughest birthday I have ever had. I was alone with two kids with not one person in this world to turn to for anything. Most people have someone. But I really had no one. Was this where I imagined myself at thirty years old? Never!

When Mom died, I realized without a doubt that the single most painful experience in life is losing those you love. This loss hurts beyond imagination. But I can also tell you one thing about this pain, "I promise you it will get better ." But only if you let it get better. In a few months, the good memories start coming to the top of your memory bank, and you smile when you think of that person. And you will feel so blessed to have had them in your life. Those memories are the one thing that no one can ever take from you. You get to keep them forever. They are yours, and you do not have to share them. But you should. Sharing them serves two purposes. It helps you keep those memories alive and vivid in your mind longer and helps the person you are sharing with get to know you better. I try to live most days, hoping I have a new memory to keep and perhaps share.

Like I said, the second thing I believe life is

about is character. That is the foundation we build from our life experiences. Hard work builds character (my children hated it when I would say that); when something makes you sad, it builds character. To get hurt builds character; to experience physical pain builds character. When something makes you happy, it builds character, and to fall in love builds character. Character is one of the features that make up and distinguish an individual. I do not think that a person can choose to change their character. It changes on its own from experiences in life.

I hope my book makes you think of a memory of yours that makes you smile. And I hope you share your memories with the people around you. Your grandchildren may not be real interested in them. But tell them anyway. One day when they are adults, they too will say, "I remember my grandma telling me this story when I was your age." And they will smile as they share it. They will remember that memory even if you think they were not listening. I hope you enjoy my book and find it to be an inspiration. And I hope every day of your life is a memorable one! Enjoy.

Hi, my name is Lola. I was the youngest of seven children, and I grew up in Nora Springs, Iowa.

It was truly a wonderful place to grow up. One of my fondest memories as a kid was a big rock in the park, Boulder Park. It has a big crack on the side. The lore/legend is the story of an Indian maiden who wept at the side of the boulder because she could not marry her true love. When she was found in the morning cold and lifeless next to the boulder, the people pointed to the fracture in the rock that had developed overnight and said the stone had felt sorry for the maiden and had broken just as her heart had. I believed the story when I was a kid, and I have no reason not to believe it today.

I spent many hours playing on this rock as a kid. Here is a picture I took in May of 2011.

This book is about my family and me and the happiness and sorrows we shared. In life, we can make many choices. But I learned when I was a child that you do not get to pick your family. And no matter what they do, if you look inside of them, you will see a part of you. Try to understand them. And love them despite their faults. We all have faults, and they are ***your family***.

"2011" I am now Fifty-six years old and have had a fantastic and interesting life. I feel like I have life lessons and life experiences of someone that has lived for one hundred years or more. Some are good, and some are not so good. But for the most part, I would not change much. If possible, live with no regrets. Regrets are something that will stay with you forever. Unfortunately, I do have a couple that I will mention later. Even though they are in the past, they still manage to keep me awake at night and most likely always will.

Mom would look at me sometimes and say words that I did not understand, but I would never forget. And some of them she only said once for a reason. She looked at me one day when I was probably about ten years old, and she said: "Lola Jean, don't you ever let anyone make you think that they are better than you. But don't you ever think that you are better than someone else either." I have had to remind myself of this statement many times. People tend to look down on you when you are part of a family that is very poor and extremely dysfunctional. Yes, my family was extremely dysfunctional. I am not sure how it is your fault that you are poor when you are a child. But society treated you very differently back then.

I am going to choose to leave last names out of most of the content of this book and some names completely. Most of this story is about my life as seen through my eyes only. These are my memories. However, I will be sharing a few things that my siblings shared with me through the years. Things that I could not remember. Although, I am very sure these things that I could not remember still played a role in where my journey would take me.

The angels in this book are the artistic talent of my granddaughters, Skyler, age 9, and Echo, age 7, and my great-grandson Kevin, age 7. Their artwork is signed. I am truly blessed to have these three angels in my life. This will show you little boys have a very different perception than little girls. Keep an eye out for these precious angels on the pages ahead.

1

∽

Our home by the river.

We lived in a house with gray shingles on the outside as well as on the roof. I remember when the stairs needed to be fixed, and a wall had to be torn out. That was when I learned that our walls had been stuffed with hay. Our house was a stable at one time. So, it was insulated with hay and straw. The windows never had storm windows or screens. We had these little screens that you would slide apart, open the window, and pull it down on top of the framed screen to let fresh air in on summer days. When it would snow and the wind would blow, there would be snow on the windowsill inside the bedroom in the morning. We had a coal heater in the living room, and a pipe went up through the floor upstairs and through the ceiling and roof. The pipe had a metal grate around it upstairs, and it was the only heat we had for three bedrooms. It was always very cold in two of the bedrooms. So, we would get up and race downstairs in the morning to get warm in front of the coal heater. All the floors were linoleum. And they were cold.

At one time, I remember a big wool rug in the middle of the living room floor. One morning I raced downstairs to get in front of the heater, and for some reason, when I got there, I fainted. I landed on that wool rug face first and had a rug burn on my cheek and a black eye. I went to school, and the teacher asked what had happened. I just said you should see the other kid, and I laughed. I am sure the teachers thought I was abused at home. Everyone in our small town knew everything about everyone. Therefore, everyone knew everything about my family for sure.

In the picture below, I am in the front of my home holding my baby niece, my mother is on the steps, and another niece and nephew are looking at my bicycle. These three little ones were my sister's children, and I will tell you more about them later. I was eleven years old in this picture, and it is quite a memory for me. I lugged that baby around like she was a toy baby doll.

Me holding my niece.

Home for me was just a couple blocks from the river. I loved the river and the millpond. When I go there today, it just floods my head with memories. It played such a huge part in all my family's lives.

We had a rope swing from the leaning tree in the picture below that we would swing out and drop into (at that time) very-clean water. On the left of the leaning tree, you can see a branch is missing. That is where we had our rope. Maybe that is why this old tree leans.

Rope-swing tree leaning by the river.

We would go outside in the morning, and Mom did not worry about us if we came home by supper time. We would play in the river, tube down the rapids, fish, catch turtles, and do so many things that all kids everywhere should get to experience. Every year thousands of gold carp would spawn up the rapids. When they spawned up the rapids, we would walk out and pick them up. Many of them were too big to pick up. But it was so fun. I had no idea at the time what their mission was, or I may not have disturbed them.

I remember my friends and me going along the

edge of the millpond with our hands in the water to catch baby leatherback turtles. They had a soft shell and a pointed nose, and they fit in the palm of my hand. We always caught them. We would play with them for a while, then turn them loose back in the water. What a great memory. And we were very fortunate that when we put our hands in the water to find them, we did not encounter a snapping turtle. We would have been missing fingers.

I could not swim, and I was way too young to be going to the river when I first started going there with friends. If I had fallen in, I would not be here. But the river was such a big part of our lives. My sisters both told me that my older siblings would take me to the river starting when I was three years old and tell me to play in the rocks and sand. They would tell me that if I went near the water, they would beat me. And I knew they would. So, I just stayed where I was supposed to stay, and they would go off to swim. They have both said they have no idea how I am alive today. But they were always stuck taking care of me. So, I do not blame them for wanting to be kids. I will express more of my thoughts on this later.

In the summer, that is just where we would go

to play. Every kid whose parents really had no idea where they were most days went to play at the river. Most parents probably cared but just did not know most of the time. My brothers would make home-made canoes with their friends out of roofing tin. You just fold the ends together, put some nails in it, bend them over, and put tar on the end. I have no idea where they got roofing tin or buckets of tar. But they did. I am not sure how many tin canoes are at the bottom of the millpond. Probably more than most of us would like to think. Does this qualify for putting metals back into the earth where they came from? Maybe, eventually. And they made homemade rafts too. We ice skated on this pond all winter. I remember when the ice would melt on the pond, there would be icebergs. My brother and his friends would ride them and go from one to another. Eventually, all the ice would go over the dam. I am not sure how we all survived our childhood. Some did not. But the river never claimed any of my siblings. For that, I am thankful.

There was a creek a couple blocks away that had a great swimming hole. It was as amazing as any swimming hole you have ever seen on TV. It was so clean you could see to the bottom of eight feet or so. It was so clear that my brothers and his friends would spear fish with homemade spears. And we would catch crawdads just for fun. A few years ago, I visited Nora Springs and went to see the creek and swimming hole, and it was dried up and overgrown with weeds. It is gone now. That, too, is very sad. Every kid should have a swimming hole like the one we had as kids.

These are just a few of the wonderful memories I have. It is so good for me to write my story as many of my childhood memories are fading.

2

How do you know you are poor?

I am not sure I would have known just how poor we were if we had lived in the country and did not go into town. We would have pancakes for breakfast and leftover cold pancakes for lunch. You just spread butter on them, sprinkle some sugar, roll them up, and eat them cold. They were good. On Saturday, Mom and Dad would usually buy some hamburger. My sister Joyce would almost always make homemade pizza or goulash. She was a wonderful cook, and we looked forward to whatever she made. But believe me, there were rarely leftovers in our house.

This was my house as a child. The photo was taken on May 17, 2011. It still has the shingles on the side to this day.

I thought that everyone took a bath in the kitchen in a washtub. When I realized most people did not, it was a real eye-opener. I do remember Grandpa always had a bathtub. I guess I never thought anything about it much. Grandpa and Grandma just had so much more than us. Maybe I just thought old people had bathtubs or something. I really don't know what I thought. I must have been around eight years old when we got running water and a bathroom with a sink, toilet, and shower. We never had a bathtub. But it was so awesome *not to go outside to go*.

It was ok at home till I would go to school. It was then I realized just how different we were from so many people. We would usually get a new pair of shoes for school, and that was it for the year. All clothes were from a garage sale or something someone gave us. I do not remember getting new clothes when I was a kid. Ever! I am sure we never did. I would get so embarrassed in school because the clothes I was wearing used to belong to someone in my school, and they knew that. My new shoes were always saddle shoes and always too big, so I could grow into them. And they would last the entire school year. I think they still make them today. I don't remember having cute shoes or tennis shoes. I think maybe we had tennis shoes for gym in school because it was required.

3

∽

My journey starts with the woman who influenced my life the most.

"My Mother"

My memories start with my mother (Betty Jane), born 6/14/1925 telling me the story of her and her four brothers standing on the porch of their little house in Rockford, Iowa. Her youngest brother was a toddler, and she was holding him. They watched as their mother walked down the road with a suitcase and never looked back. I cannot imagine the pain in their little hearts. Brings tears to my eyes just to think about it. I do believe this was the house in Rockford, Iowa. It is gone now. I can remember seeing it as a kid. It was down by the elevator in town. If you think hearing these stories when you are a child doesn't affect your life, you are wrong. Especially if you possess great empathy, they certainly do.

Betty Jane Lewis's home in Rockford, Iowa.

Mom never blamed her mother for leaving. I guess my grandpa was very jealous. Even if a traveling salesman came to the house, he would blame Grandma for messing around with him. So, she was not allowed to go anywhere. Mom always said Grandma was a prisoner in her own home. But

Grandpa was bitter and angry after she left, and Mom said it showed. So, Grandpa got a live-in housekeeper, and eventually, they married and were married till they parted in death. She was the only Grandma I ever really knew, and she was a wonderful, wonderful person. I sure do miss her sometimes. She was just one of those people that you could talk to about anything. Her name was Marie. She is the only person I can remember who ever hugged me as a child.

Grandpa made Mom wear bib overalls to school just like her brothers. She said it was so embarrassing. All she wanted was to be a girl and to feel pretty. Therefore, my mother was very young when she married her first husband, Perry. He was older than she was.

In 2019 I learned from an online family history site that when my mother's mother left, she not only left my grandpa with his five children, but she also left her son, that she had before she married my grandpa. My grandpa did not want him and gave him to the state of Iowa. How awful for this little boy? I guess he ended up in an orphanage. I had never heard of him till my niece found him online. I just cannot believe in twenty-nine years and our many hours of talking, that my mother never told me she had another brother. I do not understand how people could bury something so important in their past. Especially when it comes to family.

And so begins my story. If I stop and look at my life, most of the time, I am the luckiest person I know. I had a pretty long line of events that tried to force me in the wrong direction. Yet, I like to think I came through it all ok. It is not a miracle or anything. Anyone can do it. Sometimes the people that you meet along the way give you just enough courage, strength, and love to get you through the toughest of times. You just must gather up what you get along the way and keep moving forward.

I have said for years that I am sure God assigned an angel to me when I was born and told her to never be far away. He knew when I was born that I would have many times in my life when I would need her.

You will see throughout this journey that He was right.

My angel has followed me around my entire life. She was always there when I needed her the most. If only I had been the one following my angel, things might have been different or at least a little easier. But she followed me, and *thank God*, she never gave up on me. Lord knows I wanted to give up more than once on life. Sometimes it was almost too tough to bear. At an early age, I think I learned to cope with some things the same way I do today. If I am in a bad place in life, I always tell myself: "Where I am today is on my way to somewhere else." We tend to move forward by striving to have a better life, by defying the odds, and by welcoming good things and good people into our lives. I have always been blessed with friends and family, just as I am today.

Mom married her first husband, Perry, long enough to have two sons. William Perry (Bill) was born 2/8/1942, and Eugene Arthur (Gene) was born 3/18/1943. They were not married long when they divorced, and Mom married my dad, Elmer Leroy Sr. Mom had several more children with my dad. Jerry Allen and Joyce Alice were twins and born 4/11/1945. Connie Jo was born 10/9/1946. And Elmer Leroy Jr. was born 9/22/1950. So do the math. In eight years, my mother was married, divorced, remarried, and had six children. All I can say about that is, oh my goodness. We will talk about me later.

Mom told me that my dad hated her sons Bill and Gene from her first marriage. And his dad hated them even more. I sometimes struggle with thinking my kind father hated someone. My mother always said that my grandpa (my dad's dad) was "the meanest man that ever walked the face of the earth." If anyone mentioned him, they were the first words out of her mouth. I know I heard her say that many times in my life. Grandpa lived with my parents. He was mean to Bill and Gene, and my sister told me he hit my oldest brother Bill across the back with a 2 x 4 one time just because he felt like hitting him. And he was just a little boy. And he would buy candy for his grandchildren. But Bill and Gene could not have any. Of course, these are stories that I heard and do not remember. On May 15, 1953, my grandpa (my dad's dad) died. So, I never knew him.

In time, Mom sent Bill to live with his dad. The only problem with that was his dad did not want him either. I remember hearing the story of when Bill was locked out of his dad's house after school with no mittens or boots, and it was a cold winter day. His dad was probably at the bar drinking. The neighbor saw Bill just sitting on the steps waiting. I cannot imagine this. There are more stories like this. And they make me cry even today. How can life be so cruel to a little boy?

Then Mom sent my brother Gene to live with her father and stepmother, and they adopted him. He then became Eugene Arthur (my uncle). But to me, he was always my brother.

My brothers and sisters were the best. They were far from perfect. As we all are. Unfortunately, everyone's environment and circumstances can, and often does, take them down a path that is tough to bear. One thing I know beyond any doubt is they loved me, and I loved them. So many people journey down the same path in life and end up at extremely different destinations. This you shall see as I tell my memories of my family and share with you where my journey has taken me.

4

∽

"My oldest brother" "Wild Bill"
Born February 8th, 1942

He was called *"Wild Bill."* I really don't know when that name was given to him. My first memories of him were sometime when I was maybe five or so. He was thirteen when I was born. I believe he was gone for a couple years to live with his dad, then came back to live with us. My sister Connie told me that when Bill was a teenager, he left and hitch-hiked all over the country, and he was gone a couple years. When he returned, my mom and dad were not getting along, and Mom was in Minnesota with another man. And Dad was in Minnesota trying to find her. The five of us kids at home had no food in the house. My sister Connie said we were so hungry. Connie told me I was just a toddler, maybe three or four years old. So, Bill was sixteen or seventeen years old. Bill went to town, and he went behind the grocery store and stole food and milk from a delivery truck. He brought it home and fed us kids. Well, someone saw him, and he got in trouble. The court had no sympathy and sent him away to a boy's home. They did not care that he was trying to feed five kids. And no one cared enough to try to help him or us. They should have jailed my parents. When he got out, he was ready to change his life, and he went back to school.

But back in school, with a criminal record, was never going to work. I was told that someone stole a wallet in the boy's locker room one day, and of course, they blamed Bill. He quit school. Then they found out someone else did it. But it was too late. He would not go back to school. He really hated the world because he was pretty sure the world hated him. I think all he ever wanted was a family that loved him. I certainly do not believe that was too much to ask for from any child.

When I was around six years old, Bill got married. She was beautiful and such a lady. Her name was Betty, just like my mom. I would go stay with them, and Betty would buy me a pretty dress, shoes, and a hat to match, and we would go to church. I felt like a princess. They were so good to me. I do not know what happened to them. But Bill left with his friend, and they hitchhiked to Arkansas. When they got to Arkansas, they were tired of walking, and they stole two bicycles and road them through the town they were in. They just left them when they reached where they wanted to go. But someone saw them leave the bikes and called the law. They tried to get away, and Bill's friend pulled the sheriff's gun, and it fired and shot the sheriff's hand. Well, now they were both held and went to court. They were given fifteen years each for what happened. But Bill's friend had a family that cared, and they spent the money for an attorney. They brought their son home to Iowa. Their son never served a day in prison. But again, no one cared enough about Bill to help him. My Grandpa could have helped, but he did not. Between not being wanted and being beat, I cannot imagine how he felt. Bill spent a lot of his life in prison. Picking cotton in an Arkansas prison was probably a lot like his childhood. He spent about ten years in that horrible place. When I heard some of the stories about my brother, it truly made my heart so sad.

When Bill came home from Arkansas, I was so excited. He was my big brother, and even though I did not really know him, I wanted to know him. I remember reading an article in a magazine a few years later. They were cleaning up the prison he had been in. He told me stories. But they were really a lot worse than he said. The article said they whipped the prisoners and made them pick cotton all day. They did not always feed them. So, the prisoners would catch a rabbit by hand and cook it outside over some cotton stalks. And the authorities uncovered many remains of prisoners killed and buried on the land around the prison. I knew he had scars on his back, but his scars inside were much deeper. The story in the magazine was a real eye-opener as to what he had been through. He was kind of quiet. But I saw something in him I am sure no one else could see. It is just how I am made. I cannot help it. Inside he was a good man. The world just never gave him a chance to be good before they beat him down and made him sad and angry. We spent so much time together. He taught me to make the best Green Apple Pie you have ever eaten. We made dozens of them and would sell them to the neighbors for a couple bucks each. Bill would play the guitar and sing to me and my friends for hours on end. He played the guitar, harmonica, and the piano. He never had a lesson, but he was extremely talented. He absolutely loved to sing, just like my mom. I think maybe it helped him express who he was. Bill stayed out of prison for a few years.

Then Bill married for a second time in 1970 to a nice woman that was very well off financially. She bought him racehorses, and they traveled around some with the race circuit. But it did not work out. So, they divorced and went their separate ways.

Then, Bill met a woman that had two daughters. He never had children of his own. But he loved her girls. They never married, but they were so happy for a long time. I think they really did love one another. Or maybe they just understood and accepted one another. They had both had a tough life. They were both good people when you got to know them. And they both had a love for music. She also played the guitar and sang. So, the two of them sang and played in bands for a few years, and they really enjoyed their life together for a while. She reminded me of the country singer that lives in Tennessee, and she sure sounded just like her. She had an amazing voice. I am sure she still does.

Arrested After Robbery

Bill Perry Burgess, 22, of Marble Rock, is held in custody of Floyd County Deputy sheriff Ray Webster, right, at Nora Springs after Burgess was arrested after the robbery of First State Bank of Nora Springs Tuesday. Joe O'Rouke, 22, of Wells, Minn., was also arrested in connection with the robbery.

Article believed to have come from the Rockford Register.

Well, times got tough, and Bill could not make ends meet. So, my brother robbed a bank. It was, of course, the only bank in Nora Springs, Ia. Good grief! I could not believe my brother robbed a bank. It was a crazy time in our lives. Bill was in every newspaper and on every radio station for miles. He was arrested and put in jail in Cedar Rapids, Ia. Then he broke out of jail. Someone he knew brought him a bible, and they had carved a place for a small saw blade to be inserted under the paper on the inside of the cover. Yup, he sawed the bar and climbed out the window with the sheets tied together. Again, it was all over the news. He was on every TV channel, on the radio, and in every newspaper. They, of course, caught him. I am sure he knew when he robbed that bank that he would very possibly return to a life that he could tolerate. Maybe it was a place where he could be accepted. And maybe he did not feel so different there. I think he may even have received some respect from others there. Everyone I knew was aware that my brother robbed a bank. When Bill was sentenced to forty years in a Missouri Federal prison, it just broke my heart. His partner in this crime, that I was told was the mastermind and driver, had a family with enough money that, of course, he spent much less time in a smaller prison than my brother.

So, my husband, kids, and I would visit Bill on occasion in prison. I was the only person that ever visited him. I remember on my first visit; I was taking pictures out in front of the prison like any visitor from Iowa would. A security guard came up to me and said I could not take pictures. I thought that was so strange. I had no idea what kind of people were in this federal prison in Missouri. I did learn that there were some seriously hardened criminals in there, including people with a lot of power on the outside.

When I would visit, you were searched, had to go through a gate, put all of your belongings in a locker, then went through another gate. That was a real eye-opener. I am glad I went to visit him, though. It gave me a chance to see that he was ok. They had TV there, books, good food to eat, a dentist, and his health was taken care of. He loved to read, and he read every page of the Bible, Old, and New Testament, more than once. He was a great believer in God. Bill absolutely loved God. I think he prayed a lot. And I am sure God did listen because He gave Bill peace.

At Christmas, Bill could receive a package of goodies. I would shop for the very-specific items that the prison would allow and send them to him. Nuts, dried fruit, packaged candy, etc. He would be so excited to get them because very few inmates received anything from someone who cared. And he would tell me about how he shared the goodies with his friends. It made him feel like there was someone that really cared. And I did. He was my brother, and I loved him.

He served ten years there, and at that time, I was married and had a couple small children and a home. So, he was paroled to live with me when he got out. It was so wonderful at first. He was content to sit by the river in our backyard and watch nature. He would look at me and get very quiet, then tell me to listen. I would look at him and say, "what am I listening to"? Then he would say, "listen to that beautiful bird sing." It was music to him. A kind of music I was still too young to understand. I was busy working, taking care of my children, and running a household. He loved life. But when he was no longer content, he got very restless. We had a few discussions, and he knew I disapproved of his friends.

One day I came home from work, and he had some friends in my house that I did not approve of. Then another person stopped over that was known all over town as a local drug dealer. I asked my brother to come to the kitchen. I was so angry. I slammed my fist so hard on the counter I thought I broke my hand. I screamed for him to get them out of my house. They heard me and stood up and walked towards the door. I went up to the guy that was known to be a drug dealer. I pointed my finger in his face and said, "Get out of my house, and don't you ever come back." Everyone cleared out. I remember someone saying to me I should not have done that because they were bad people. At that point, I did not care. My children were young, and it was my job to protect them. I pitied anyone that got in the way. I was not afraid of any of them. I never saw any of them ever again.

But I knew what was coming. He came home less and less, and finally, he and I had words, and he left. He called me one night not long after, collect from Las Vegas, NV. He took his veterans check and went to Vegas to get rich quick. But his call was to tell me he had no money, or food, or a place to sleep, and no way to get back to Iowa. I called his parole officer, and he had him picked up, and he returned to prison for a while. I heard he was somewhere in a prison in Wisconsin.

After a few years, he got out, and he lived in a little apartment in Northwood, Iowa. I did not see him or speak to him during this time, but I heard he was content those last few years. Then he got sick and went to the VA hospital for his final days. So, I went to see him and brought him a bag of fresh fruit. He loved fresh fruit. (You know, something that most people take for granted) and we sat outdoors and visited for a long time and ate fresh fruit. We made amends. I am glad I did that. But he died a few days later, on 8/5/2003, in the V.A. hospital, lonely and sad. My brother Gene and my sister Connie were with him. He was sixty-one years old, and I was forty-eight years old. I could not believe the sadness that flooded my whole being at this time. My goodness, when would the sadness end?

Bill and I when we made amends at the VA hospital.

I remember thinking, I wish God would have given a little less to me and had picked Bill up and carried him a little farther up his hill in life. His hill in life was just too steep. I would still have been just fine. He could have done so much in life if just given the chance.

In 2016, a woman friended me on Facebook that married a childhood friend of my brother Bills. She wrote to me to say she was thankful that my brother made it possible for her to be married to her wonderful husband. She told me that my brother Bill had saved her husband's life when they were kids. They were ice fishing. Her husband fell through the ice. As he was sinking to the bottom, my brother Bill hooked his coat with his fishing pole and started pulling him up. Then another boy with them did the same thing, and they pulled him out of the water. What an amazing story for someone I have never met or spoken one word to, to share with me. It made me smile. My brother bill was a good person in so many ways that most people just never got to see.

Here he is tying his ice skates on the millpond. Not much for winter clothes in our house. I doubt he rarely had winter gloves or a hat as a kid. I remember I didn't always have them. I have no idea who would have taken this picture.

Life was not good to him. He was always so beaten down and just could never rise above the pain and hurt. The world missed out on a great guy. And that great guy missed out on a good life. He sure was a handsome man.

I still miss you, Bill, every day.

See you again someday,

Love, your sis (he always called me Sis), Lola

5

～

Grandpa and Grandma Lewis

We would go to Grandpa and Grandma's every Sunday. My mother's father and stepmother. So, did all my aunts and uncles and cousins. On Sunday, Grandma always made roast beef or fried chicken with potatoes and gravy and usually corn for everyone. I still wonder how she cooked for all of us just about every Sunday. There would have been a total of eight or ten adults and most likely twelve kids. She was amazing. Grandma always made a cake too. All of us kids would try to get to Grandpa first when he got his cake. Whoever got there first would get his frosting. He would scrape it off his cake and put it on your plate. He had diabetes. So, he never ate the frosting.

My grandpa had very-strict rules in his house. You had to be quiet if Gunsmoke or the news was on. Or you would get scolded by Grandpa. And for some reason, no one ever wanted to be scolded by Grandpa. I don't think he was mean to us, but you listened when he talked. We were taught respect for sure.

My grandma was a fabulous cook and, beyond any doubt, made the best oatmeal cookies with raisins and walnuts in the world. And she was funny. I have a dimple in my chin. She used to grab my chin and say, "a dimple in the chin means the devil is within." Then she would hug me. She really meant that I was just always a high-spirited kid. I think I was always full of life, probably from the time I was born. I did not know it then, but I am positive my grandma did.

My grandma was interesting. She had these little papers and a can of velvet tobacco, and she smoked. She rolled her own cigarettes for as long as I could remember. But her most favorite thing in the whole world to do was play cards. She would play rummy for hours and hours with anyone that would play with her. If I stayed overnight, we would play till all hours of the night. And it was common to walk in, and she would be playing solitaire.

Or she would be crocheting with thread. She would make an entire tablecloth out of thread. I learned to crochet. But I never had the patience she did for such tasks as a tablecloth out of thread that was eight feet long or more. She would crochet all these different things for the square window in the front door too. One had flowers, but most of all, I remember, one was a peacock. It was so pretty. I always wondered how on earth she could do that. She was amazing to me in so many ways. Just like a grandma should be. I loved her so much. She was the true definition of a grandma. Always happy to see everyone and always a hugger. I think that might be where I learned to think hugs were like vitamins. They make you feel good.

Grandma had an organ, and she would play and sing all the time. Their dog would sit next to her and howl when she played. She was of German heritage, and she would sing Silent night in English, then in German. I remember just being mesmerized. It was so beautiful. If only I could hear her one more time. I used to think if I pulled that memory up in my mind, I could hear her. But it has faded over the years. It's just not as vivid of a memory as it used to be. If only we had been able to record such beautiful moments in our lives. If only.

I asked Grandma one time if Grandpa looked at other girls. She said, "Yup! When they stop looking, you better start worrying." I was very young and didn't quite understand.

We had a rope swing in a barn across the street from my grandpa's house on the farm. The barn was the only thing there. No one lived there. We would swing in the haymow and land on the floor below in a pile of hay. I remember another time we went to Grandpa's in the winter and walked out the door up in the haymow of Grandpa's barn onto the snow. And we would slide down it. It was a blast. I now realize how dangerous it was. If any of us had fallen through, it would have taken days to dig us out. It had to be fifteen feet or higher against the barn. There she was, as always, my very own angel. She was always there to protect me. Maybe most kids have one. Maybe all kids have one. I really have no idea. But I am convinced I have always had an angel. Why me? Why was I special or important? Did I have a purpose? I have some ideas that I will mention later. Always there for me, keeping me safe and feeling loved. When I felt her presence, I think I was very calm and content. I am sure of it, even though, at the time, I had no idea what made me feel this way. I just know I felt that way sometimes.

6

My brother/uncle, Gene. Born March 18th, 1943

My brother Gene, who was adopted by my grandpa and grandma, had a totally different life than we did. Grandpa lived on a farm, and they had lots of food to eat, and Gene had a nice house to live in with his very own room and his own bed. Grandma spoiled him, and he had a pretty good life. But you must remember that my grandpa had very-strict rules in his house. If you did not behave when you were at his house, you would be in trouble, and when Grandpa scolded you, you would absolutely feel bad.

Gene's life was not always good. But he was doing the best he could. Gene was making his way in life. What can I say? He was gay. At that time, in a small town in Iowa, being gay was like having two heads. Seriously. When he was old enough to move away, he did and lived in Los Angeles and several other big cities over the years. He told me one time that he auditioned for a part in the movie Planet of The Apes. He had an awesome, very professional portfolio of pictures of himself that he showed me, and he really was very handsome. Whenever he came home for a visit, I would be so excited. He would take my girlfriends and me out for fun. He cooked for us and taught us all the newest fashions for makeup and clothes in the big city. He was so fun. He was one of the most fun people I have ever known. And he was kind. Kindness is a quality that many people never have.

One time, Gene, I, and some of my friends were at the bowling alley. Some rough and tough guy that was underage decided to beat up my brother simply because he was gay. I watched as this person beat my brother to the point I could hardly recognize who he was. And no one would help him. And he would not hit back because he was older, and he would have gone to jail for hitting a minor. The guy knew that when he started the fight. It broke my heart. He did not do anything to deserve what was done to him. He was good and kind. He would give anyone the shirt off his back. He took in more people and animals over the years than he could afford to feed most of the time. He gave and gave and gave in his life. And he never asked for anything in return but acceptance. That just could not happen in a small town in Iowa or anywhere, for that matter, back then. He left soon after that. He finally spent many years in Cedar Rapids, Ia., and Des Moines, Ia. He married a woman twice and tried to change his life. But it did not last.

So, he tried to visit a couple times a year. Otherwise, we rarely heard from him. It made Grandma very sad.

When Grandpa died, my husband at the time and I went to get Gene in Des Moines, Iowa. I met some of his friends, and he really did live a different life than anyone else I had ever known.

Gene did return to Mason City, Ia., for the last few years of his life with his partner of many years. He was poor but never complained. He would still cook and feed anyone that showed up and was hungry. He died in the VA hospital, lonely and sad. It is hard for me to think he is gone sometimes. I did not see him much the last couple years, and he was cremated and had no funeral. His partner was not nice about it and would not let any of us have his ashes or any of his belongings. So, when his partner passed away, his family took everything of any value. They had a lot of beautiful antique furniture. But they did finally let my sister Connie have his ashes.

In 2020, my sister Connie and I spread his ashes on my brother Bill's grave and poured water till they were gone. Shhhhhh, I am not sure you are supposed to do that. That is where he belonged. We thought about putting him on Grandma and Grandpa. But Bill was his full blood brother, and I hope they are together with peaceful hearts and Jesus.

Gene was funny, had a great spirit, but carried a great sadness in his heart. I know the story of his sadness, and it is not something I will share with anyone.

I did not get to say goodbye and tell him how much he meant to me in my life. He always told me how proud he was of me for getting away and making a different life for myself and my kids. And he knew it was not always easy for any of us kids. I am confident he knows today how I felt. He was my brother, and I always loved him no matter what happened. Gene left us on 1/3/2008. He was sixty-five, and I was fifty-three years old.

I miss you, brother, and I think of you often. Oh my, my heart aches some days. I write this through tears.

Love you forever, your sister, Lola

7

The Twins, Joyce Alice and Jerry Allen, Born April 11th, 1945

"My Brother Jerry"

My brother Jerry was the perfect brother, son, husband, father, and person. To me, anyway. He left home when he was sixteen years old and never returned except for an occasional visit. He settled about one hundred miles away in Marshalltown, Iowa. So, we did not see him much. Despite our home life, he was good, kind, whistled all the time, smiled, and walked with a beat in his step. No matter where he went, everyone loved him. In my eyes, he was just an amazing person. I think I admired how he rose above the life we had as kids and smiled. It was tough on Jerry as a kid.

But moving to Marshalltown made it possible for Jerry to meet the love of his life. They got married, settled in a small town in Central Iowa, and had a little girl Tracy Lynn born 8/16/1965. He adored his family. They were happy and loved each other so much you could see it when they looked at each other. You could feel it in the room. Jerry was by far the single most positive force in my life as a child. He started with an empty cup, and he filled it up. It was never half empty or half full. He loved life, and he lived life. I would go stay with them sometimes. We would play outside, eat dinner as a family, and just spend time together. It was so nice. A happy family! I never wanted to go home.

But Jerry was sick. He had ulcerative colitis. When Jerry was twenty-two years old, he got sick because he had lost so much blood. So, he ended up in the hospital and was given a blood transfusion. They told us that the blood that was given to him came from someone that had hepatitis. My brother Jerry got a staph infection from that blood, and he died on May 12th, 1967, at twenty-two years of age. I was just twelve years old. It was so sad. I was twelve years old, and my hero, my rock, the one person that I could see hope through his eyes, had died with no warning. I could not prepare for this, and I did not even get to say goodbye. I think I hated life for the first time. He was taken from me and everyone that loved him so much. I remember being so sad. And it left a big hole in my heart. But, in time, it healed.

Jerry worked at a big factory, and everyone he

knew was at his funeral. The church was full, even in the isles. Many people stood outside the church because there was no room. Everybody loved him. I was not sure if his wife would get through it. She wanted to go with him. But life goes on, right?

After Jerry died, we kind of lost track of his wife and daughter. She moved on with her life and ended up marrying again and having a couple more children. Jerry's daughter Tracy told me later in life that her home life with her stepdad was not good and that he ruined her life.

I made a trip to see my brother's daughter Tracy in hospice in July of 2016. On my trike. I didn't really start riding till I was sixty years old. It was yellow when I bought it. I had it painted Merlot Pearl.

You want to see this country? Take the top down on your car or get a bike. It's beautiful!

Tracy was so excited to see me. She told me her only wish for years was to be with her dad. She lost him when she was two years old.

Tracy Lynn passed away on July 9th, 2016, at fifty-one years of age. I pray to God that the first thing she was able to do when she passed was to be wrapped in her Daddy's arms. It is truly what she had longed for most of her life. Her life had so much sadness. I pray she is with my brother and has a peaceful heart. Everyone's heart deserves peace.

"My Sister Joyce"

As I said, my sister Joyce and my brother Jerry were twins. When he died, I think a piece of her soul died. I think it is just that way with twins. And I do not believe the hole in her heart ever healed.

Joyce raised two wonderful daughters and an amazing son. Two girls and a boy, but she was never married. Again, back then, you might as well have had a third eye or something. Society looked at you differently and condemned you for having a child and not being married. And she had three. I think she became angry from loneliness. There is nothing worse than to feel lonely or alone in the world with more on your plate than you can possibly handle. I know this firsthand. But today, having children and not being married is accepted by most of society. I am sure her life could have been so different today.

On January 26th, 1961, Kelly Marie was born, Joyce's first child. I was 5 ½ years old. Somewhere around this time, I think we got a phone in our house. Joyce and her kids always lived with us. So, Kelly was instantly more like my baby sister and still is to this day. Kelly and I are very close. I remember when Kelly was a baby, she had croup. That poor baby would cough and cough and cough. One day she coughed so much that she stopped breathing. My sister dialed 911, and poor baby Kelly turned blue right before my eyes. But the paramedics arrived, and they put oxygen on her, and she turned pink again. I was six years old at the time, and I remember being positively terrified. I guess maybe she had an angel looking out for her just as I do. Or maybe my angel helped her. For years, Kelly would sometimes make noises at night, and you had to roll her over on her tummy so she could breathe more easily. I learned to listen and do this at a very young age. And I did it once when she came to stay with me when she was about ten years old. I heard her in the night, and I went in the living room where she was on the sofa and rolled her over. I have always had that ear for a child when I am sleeping. I was born with it, I guess.

I remember when she first met her husband. She asked him to come with her to meet her Aunt Lola and her husband. He said no way. Little did he know I was a year younger than him. My husband, my kids, and I spent many weekends at Kelly and Marv's in the country. We had so much fun! Kelly is such a good person. She is kind, loving, and nice. It just doesn't get much better than that woman. And, oh my goodness, when my family and I stayed with them, she and I would stay up and talk for hours after everyone went to bed (just like Mom and I would one day), and we would laugh till our sides hurt. We grew up together and shared so many memories. Kelly has been married for thirty-nine years. Together with her husband, they raised two great boys. However, on December 15th, 1995, Kelly's husband had a major stroke, and their life changed forever. He was forty-one years old and would never work again. Kelly was a homemaker who soon found herself working to see them through a tough couple years. Their two boys were fifteen and eighteen years old at the time. But they are great boys. They all made it through these times; the boys married terrific women and gave Kelly and Marv three wonderful grandchildren that they enjoy very much. Thus, the story continues as they, too, are raising some great kids. In some ways, Kelly's life was harder than most. But I think the good in her life outweighs the bad by far!! She, like my brother Jerry, rose above the tough times and made life good. As it should be.

Joyce's son Scott David was born December 13, 1962. I was seven years old. So, he was instantly more like my baby brother. Scott and I, too, had a very close relationship. Scott had some troubles with speech from the time he was a little boy, and he didn't listen very well. Joyce would tell him to do something when he was just a little boy, and he would not even acknowledge that she said something. Of course, she would hit him for not listening. My sister Joyce was a hitter. After a couple years of this, the school discovered he was tone-deaf. He could not hear some tones. If you were behind him or in front of him, he might not hear you talk at all. But he would always hear an airplane go over. Poor little boy. He loved to lay on the ground and watch airplanes.

Scott always struggled with self-esteem and self-worth. I think maybe because of his speech problem when he was little and not having a dad. All boys and girls need a dad. But boys likely need one just a little more than girls. Not much, just a little.

Well, Scott grew up, got married to a woman against all our advice, and had two daughters. I'm sorry, but his wife was not a good person at all. And I really do my best not to judge others. They lived with me for a while before their daughters were born, and she was so filthy and disgusting. Well, they struggled, and when the carnival came to town somewhere around 1986 or so, they went to work for them and left town with the carnival. They left their daughters with my sister Joyce, and she raised them and eventually adopted them. But more sorrow was to come. Scott was found dead hanging in a tree in Ola, Arkansas, on 8/30/1992.

I cannot, nor would I want to imagine how Joyce felt when she got that call. I cried so hard when I heard Scott died. I almost fell on the floor. My first thoughts were Scott grew up without a dad, and he never had a chance in life. Not a chance. I was so angry he died like he did. His life was so hard, and I was sad beyond comprehension. Really, I was sad beyond what most humans can only imagine. He was like my little brother. When would this sadness end? And in my heart, I believe his wife knew why he was hanging in a tree. To my knowledge, that woman has never even reached out to her own two daughters she left behind. But my sister was poor and not able to hire someone to investigate what happened. The funeral was so sad. The sadness in my heart was so, so, so painful. I could not fathom the pain in my sister's heart. They say the lord does not give us more than we can handle. Well, I am telling you, I needed a heart of stone to withstand all the sadness. When would it end?

Joyce's youngest child, a daughter, Robbyn Ann, was born 3/14/1966. I was almost eleven years old. Again, they lived with us. So, she was like my little sister. We were close, but now I was eleven, and three little kids were getting to be a bit much. Joyce told me she was engaged to Robbyn's father, and my mother broke it off. Then my mother took him to court for a lump sum child support. She let Joyce have a little of the money, and she took the rest. He was a farmer, and they really loved each other. He was ready to give my sister and her two kids a good life. One she could only have ever dreamed of. But his mother and my mother would not let that happen. I am guessing maybe at that time, my sister lost hope. Robbyn grew up and married and had a son and a daughter. Her marriage ended, but she raised two great kids and now has grandchildren of her own. Robbyn has worked hard to provide for herself and her kids. She has done a very good job rising above her obstacles in life.

I remember one time I was babysitting the three kids when I was just a kid. Scott came in the house screaming. He had gotten in a bee's nest, and they were inside his clothes. I really had no idea what to do, so I grabbed him and ran up the stairs, and I put him in the shower. I took his clothes off to get rid of them. I could not hit them all. All that mattered was to get them off him. I don't know how I thought of the shower, but it worked.

Joyce not only had three kids of her own to take

care of 24\7. She was stuck taking care of me most of the time too. My parents were not home most nights. I am sure she resented being saddled with kids all the time and no time for herself. The absolute worst thing she ever did to me probably started when I was four or five years old. Joyce would tell me to go upstairs to bed, and on the way up, she would tell me that the boogie man was going to get me. And when I would sit on the stairs and cry, she would threaten to spank me if I did not get up to bed. So, I would cry all the way up the stairs and lay in bed terrified. If I had not gone upstairs to bed, she would have spanked me or hit me. I must have believed the boogie man was terrible for me to be so scared. I remember it like it was yesterday. I was sure he was real. To this day, if there is no one else in the house, I leave a light on or have night lights everywhere. I am absolutely afraid of the dark when I am alone. I still have not really figured out who the boogie man is. But I am sure he is not nice. Otherwise, why would he want to get little kids?

Yes, Joyce hit me sometimes. Back then, if kids did not do what they were told, it was pretty common for them to get hit. At least in my house, it was a normal way of life. That is just the way it was. One time she wanted me to do the dishes, and I refused because it was not my turn. She backhanded me, and I flew across the kitchen, hit the cupboard, and fell on the floor. I am not kidding. I was airborne. She was six foot one inches tall and a big woman. If she hit you, you would absolutely feel it. And you really did not want her to do it again. And yes, I did those dishes.

I do not blame her for hitting. She was an angry woman in those days. And her only example was my mom, whom I am pretty sure hit Joyce often.

We had an old gas cookstove that you had to light the burners and oven with a match. I am sure most people did this. But one day, my sister Joyce was lighting the oven, and it blew up and shot out flames. All her hair on her head was burnt, as well as her eyelashes and eyebrows. I guess she was lucky that is all that happened. She could have started on fire. I think we got a new stove after that.

I recall Joyce had a boyfriend and his guy friend over one time, and they were drinking beer. Mom was drinking beers with them, and they were having a great time. I was sent to bed, and I crawled in my mom's bed to sleep. The guy friend of my sister's boyfriend came upstairs to use the bathroom, then he sat on the edge of the bed and was talking to me. My mother came up those stairs, and I thought she went insane and that she was going to kill him. She went crazy. She was screaming at the top of her lungs, and she threw them both out of our house. I did not get it. She was absolutely a wild woman. I was scared to death myself. He just talked to me, and that was it. I get it now. Again, I am sure someone was watching out for me and sent my mother up those stairs. There she was again, never ever leaving my side. Why was I so blessed and protected? Why me?

Sometimes Joyce worked for a neighbor a couple blocks away that had his own business. Joyce would help him roof houses. He knew how poor we were. She could carry a bundle of shingles up the ladder, and a lot of men couldn't do that. She was never afraid to work hard. She would have done well today. She would have worked hard and made a good life for herself and her three children in a society that would have accepted her. I am sure of that.

Joyce was also an amazing artist. She could literally draw anything. She entered an art contest once and won. But going off to school was not something that was promoted in our family. She drew people or scenery with rivers, houses, flowers, etc. There really was nothing she could not draw perfectly.

Joyce and I spent about three hours talking on the phone about a year before she died. It was a very painful call. You see, while my mother left this world as my best friend, my sister Joyce hated our mother. She told me about the time Mom left dimes for all the kids on the table to go to town for a treat when Joyce was a little girl. But when Joyce took one, Mom told her she did not have permission. Our mother burned all of Joyce's fingers on the stove for taking a dime. None of the other kids were in trouble. And she ruined Joyce's life by breaking off the engagement to Robbyn's dad for money. She told me that the reason she never went to see my mom the last few years she was alive was because she was told she was not welcome. We cried and cried on this phone call. I am sure my eyes were swollen for days after that call. I told her I was so sorry that while we had the same birth mother, my life with my mother was very different from hers. Mostly be-cause my mom had just me for a long time, and she married my stepdad, that gave her a good life. That was a long and painful phone call, and we cried for most of it. Joyce and I were born in a different generation. She was ten years old when I was born. I remember feeling so sad for her. My heart just broke hearing about how our mother was so cruel to her. I was told that Joyce left a journal when she died that has many horror stories in it. My niece told me I needed to read it, and I told her that I would never read it. I truly have had enough sadness for one lifetime. Adding more, currently in my life, does not serve a purpose for me or anyone else.

Joyce did marry someone that had four kids he was raising alone, and that is a horror story that I hope is never written. I heard one of his sons will spend the rest of his life in prison for what he did to his own two daughters when they were just little girls. And that was not the worst of that family. Most of the memories that family shares need to die and be buried with them. They would haunt anyone that knows them. And yes, they haunt me.

So, needless to say, Joyce's kids, Kelly, Scott, and Robbyn, could not wait to leave home once Joyce moved in with her future husband. I often wondered if she regretted moving in with him and eventually marrying him. There is no doubt in my mind today that she really regretted ever meeting her husband and his kids.

But diabetes was not good to Joyce. She had lost several toes to surgery and eventually lost one leg to the knee. I remember when I went to Iowa when she was having surgery to amputate her leg off to the knee. I was crying as she went into surgery and asked her if when she went home if she would eat better and take better care of herself? She said she would. But a year or so later, I saw her at her daughter Kelly's house, and she ate several deserts. She just really believed that those shots fixed everything even after what she had been through. Or maybe she was so sad that she didn't care. It made me so sad. She was not well for a long time before she left this earth.

March 24, 2015, my sister Joyce went to be with her twin brother Jerry, her son Scott, her father, her mother, her brothers Bill, Gene, and Elmer Jr, our nephew Tom, our niece Tracy, and all our grandparents. In her final days, I wrote this for her:

Since I was a young girl, I always thought you seemed so much older than me. I knew this day would come. But I never in my wildest dreams expected to feel the way I do.

It seems so long ago that we were big sister and little sister. Now we are just sisters.

Some would say our life was tough. But it made us who we are. And inside, we are good people.

Together we could move mountains back then. But today you are too tired to move mountains.

Even if you are tired, I will move a mountain for you. And I will sit you on top close to God so He can protect you.

Remember, you are my sister, and I will always love you, Lola.

At times, I am sure that my older siblings hated me because they were stuck with me all the time. They mostly raised me. My parents were in the bar. And after my dad died, Mom started seeing someone, and she was gone a lot. I don't blame my brothers and sisters for hating me. They wanted to be kids, not raise a kid. But deep down, we all loved each other. And we held on to each other to survive. Truth be told, my sister Joyce had the hardest life of anyone I have ever known on this earth. It had so much sorrow and pain. But she loved her kids, grandkids, and great-grandkids like no other person on this earth. Her love for them was beyond extraordinary.

8

∽

My Sister, Connie Jo, Born October 9th, 1946

My sister Connie was nine years old when I was born. I was probably most like Connie. She was a tomboy and loved to be outdoors. I never really knew her when I was little because she left when I was about four years old. But we did get close after she got married and are very close now.

Connie told me when she was thirteen, she went to school and told the principal that she did not want to go home anymore because of the drinking and the violence. She told him she was going to run away. So, the principal called social services, and they placed Connie in a home with an elderly woman so my sister could take care of her. This woman lived about a block and a half away from our house. The lady was a retired elderly schoolteacher in a wheelchair and needed someone to take care of her and cook and clean. Connie said her name was Carrie. So, my sister lived with her, took care of her, and went back and forth to school from there. Connie told me she was very happy there. She had to come right home from school and take care of Carrie's needs, clean the house if needed, and do her homework. Then she could play outside if it wasn't time for her to prepare supper for the two of them. And at night, they would play cards. This woman was so wonderful to my sister. I think she gave her hope and likely made her feel loved. Connie said it was a good place to be, and she didn't have a desire to come home much. She had a warm bed and food, and it was a much better life than being at home. And she paid my sister a few dollars each week for taking care of her. One day Carrie had a heart attack, and Connie called the doctor. After that, Carrie went to the nursing home. Connie said she went to visit her all the time till she passed away.

Between the anger, hate, fighting, and drinking, our house just was not a great place to live.

Connie said when Carrie went to the nursing home, she came home, and she stayed home for a month or so because, during this time, our mother was depressed and thought she was worthless. Connie felt she needed to be there for her. Connie said during this time, she had to go rescue Mom eight or ten times when someone would call and say Mom was sitting on the edge of the bridge on the highway crying and ready to jump. Connie said no one else would go, so she would walk across town and convince Mom that we needed her and talk to her till she could get her off the edge of the bridge. She would then walk her home over a mile, undress her, and put her to bed. Mom was always intoxicated when this happened. So, Connie was not home for very long when she asked Grandma and Grandpa if she could live with them, and they said yes. So, my sister Connie then went to live on the farm. She just could not live with the drinking and violence that we lived with.

Connie married a year or so later, when she was sixteen years old, at "The Little Brown Church." She had two sons and was with her husband till he passed. They lived in Rockford, Ia. It was only ten miles away, and they had a car. So, she and her husband would come to visit every week. And sometimes I would go stay with them. I can guarantee you, there was no drinking in her home and no violence.

As I said, Connie and her husband Gary had two wonderful boys. William Leroy, born January 17th, 1964, and Robert Allen, born April 28th, 1969. Connie was most likely the most amazing mother I have ever known. She taught her boys to fish, trap, and hunt, and they have done this their entire lives. They bow hunted, hunted with black powder guns, and sold a lot of furs during trapping season. I would guess there were times when they had thirty guns in their house. Sometimes when they hunted, her sons got first shot, and she got second. She said many times she did get to shoot and would get what they were shooting at. Connie's husband got sick and was unable to work when her boys were young. He was never able to take the boys to do these things. So, she did. I am sure there is a special place in heaven for my sister Connie. I remember often thinking that I was sure she had a place at the right hand of God. She had to be a saint. Her whole life, she gave and gave and has never ever asked for anything in return, even to this day. She truly is an amazing example for us all.

Connie and me at Christmas in 2020. She was so excited I bought her a Christmas sweatshirt.

I lived in Rockford, only a block away from Connie, when my kids were young for a while. She would take her boys and my son at 5:00 A.M., trapping for animals every day during trapping season. She was my son's most favorite person in the world when he was a little boy. He just loved spending time with her. Of course, she would let him drive her car in the fields when he was just ten years old. When we lived close, he would walk up to her house and just sit and talk with her and her husband. They were very good to him, and they were also very good *for* him.

And it was during this time that Connie and I became close. We lived close when Mom died. So, she was there to see me through a very tough time in my life. Very possibly one of the toughest times I would ever endure.

Connie lost her husband January 9th, 2003. They had been married for almost forty years. It was a tough life because of his illness. But she loved him despite his illness and was devoted to him till the day he passed. Actually, Connie's devotion to her husband has never faded for one day in the eighteen years he has been gone. She still talks of him with great love in her heart. You can see it when she talks.

July 26th, 2015, my sister Connie lost her oldest son William. Just a little more than four months after losing our sister Joyce whom she was very close to and talked to on the phone all the time. William was fifty-one years old. He fought a horrible battle with alcohol and drugs that he just could not win. Both of my sisters and my sister-in-law all lost a son. My heart ached for her when her son passed. This is something I cannot comprehend. I cannot fathom losing a child. When people I know have lost a child, I have wondered, how do you get out of bed the next day, how do you keep breathing, how do you go on with life? I do not truly know that I could imagine waking up in the morning and not being able to talk to any of my children. I pray to God I never ever experience this in my life.

But as, my brother Jerry and my dad, Connie, had ulcerative colitis. She was sick for many years and then eventually had to have her colon removed. The medicine she took for so many years has been very hard on her bones, and they break easily. She has had a few broken bones just from doing nor-

Connie and I at the river in June of 2019.

mal household activities. And she has diabetes, as we all do. And it has not been good to her. She takes insulin shots every day, and her health is not the best. She has had a very, very hard life. But as I said, she never complains. It is 2020, I am sixty-five years old, and she is all I have left of my family.

Connie lives in a little apartment alone with her cat in Rockford, Iowa. She had a dog, Baily, that was truly her best friend at the time. But she lost her in 2019. She recently told me that her wish is to be cremated and buried next to her husband and that Baily's ashes are to be buried with hers. She still talks about Baily all the time. She really misses her friend.

It dawned on me recently, March 2020, that my sister Connie has never seen a mountain, she has never seen the ocean, she has never flown in an airplane, she has never eaten at a five-star restaurant, she has never had a brand new car, she has never dyed her hair, she has never had her nails done or had a pedicure, she has never had name brand clothes, shoes, or a purse, she has never been to the theatre, she has never been on a cruise, she has never been to a tropical island, and she has no complaints about her life. I sit here staring at this screen as I comprehend what I just wrote. I have done all those things. That is tough for me to think about. But as I write this, I remember when I was young imagining doing most of those things, and they were just a wish or a dream. I guess maybe I chased my dreams, and I caught some of them. I don't remember my sisters ever saying they wished or dreamed of things other than what they had.

I visited Connie March 12–14, 2020, and we

discussed that she will likely go to a nursing home in the next few months. I bought her a photo frame to hold all her grandchildren and great-grandchildren and a photo album to put all her pictures in to take to the nursing home with her. I bought her new covers for her walker. The pattern on the material has hearts on it, and it says Jesus loves me. This is so hard for me. But I made her promise me that she is going there to live, not to die. I need her to stick around for a while. Lord knows I need her way more than she needs me. My prayer right now is to go see her when I retire, rent a convertible, pick her up, and go riding. Oh my, we would have so much fun. I pray to God that we get to do this.

It is August 23rd, 2020, today. We are living with the pandemic of Covid-19 and the battle of the most important presidential election in history. This election is going to change our country forever, no matter what the outcome. I won't go into what my thoughts are on the state of this country right now. But I will say, to me, it is so sad.

So, with Covid-19, Connie can't go to the nursing home. So, she is very isolated from the world and very alone. I try to call at least once a week, and we usually talk for at least a couple hours. But our talks can never replace the talks she had with our sister Joyce. They were so close in age that they actually lived together during their childhood. They enjoyed life together as kids as well, and they shared the sorrows of their childhood. Connie misses Joyce terribly every single day.

June 2021, Connie is still in her apartment, and the pandemic is starting to get better. She has fallen a couple times, and some days are better than others. I assume she will be in a nursing home by fall. But we will see.

Christmas 2021. Connie is actually doing much better. A few months ago, her son went to check on her, and she was so confused that she did not know what she was doing at all. He called an ambulance, and she was put in the hospital. She was on the wrong medication and had an infection.

January 2022. The pandemic is still very bad. The virus has mutated a few times, and people are still getting sick and dying. This country and this world are both in big trouble.

February 21, 2022. Connie told me she has fallen three times in the last couple weeks and has had to push her emergency button to get help getting up. Luckily, she has not broken anything. She is now talking about going to the nursing home in March or April of 2022. I sent her a new Robe this week to wear when she goes.

March 6, 2022. I had a tough week and cried a couple times. My sister Connie will go to the nursing home next week. I know she is afraid, and it will be very hard for her. I will go see her in April. I want to wait for her to adjust and give her something to look forward to. She is all I have left of my family.

March 8, 2022. My sister Connie went to the nursing home to live today. At 8:30 this morning, she called my niece Kelly and said she did not want to go. I called her the next day. I was so excited because when she was taken to her room, she knew her roommate. My nephew said the two of them were talking, laughing, and joking around. And she told me she played cards the first night. I cried again, happy tears. It warms my heart that she will not be alone, and she will have people to talk to.

2009 with my sisters, Joyce (in front), Connie and me.

9

∾

My Brother, Elmer Jr., Born September 22nd, 1950

My youngest brother was named after my dad Elmer. His name was Elmer Jr., but we called him Junior. As we got older, Junior and I would become good friends. He was the closest in age to me, and he never quit picking on me till he left this earth to join his maker. I remember so much about him. One year for Christmas, I got an A.M. transistor radio. I loved it. Well, a few weeks after Christmas, my brother Jr. took it apart to see how it worked and never got it back together. He was good at taking things apart. But he was not always good at putting things back together again.

Junior and his friends would ask me to pitch for them, and they would just hit long balls in the field behind three or four houses. Of course, I would pitch. But one day, one of those boys hit a line drive right into my leg. I thought my leg was broken. So, I hobbled the block and a half or so home, crying all the way. They went on to hit balls. Well, guess what? Even though I was pretty sure I was not going to live, I did. I was maybe eleven years old. I am sure Mom or my sister told me to quit acting like a baby and go outside and play.

One time Junior and I were the only two left at the table, and we were horsing around. So, we started shooting mashed potatoes at each other. He was using a spoon, and I was using a fork. Well, my fork flew out of my hand and stuck in my brother's head. Honest to goodness, it did. It was sticking straight up. It wasn't in very deep, but the head bleeds awful, and I was sure he was going to die. I ran to the stairs and cried and cried. That is where I always went to cry. Mom took him to the doctor, and he was fine.

Junior would get picked on in school terribly as

I did because we were poor and because of whom our family was. It seemed to me at an early age in life that in my small town, you were judged, and you were labeled into one of two categories. To me, these categories were rich or poor. We were so poor that, to me, the entire rest of the town was rich. I am serious. I think if you ask anyone that remembers my family, they might say we were a pathetic, poor, and extremely dysfunctional family. It wasn't till I was a mature adult that I realized the riches we had.

Junior and I used to jump out of the upstairs window onto a mattress in the backyard. That was fun. Again, I am not sure why we didn't get terribly hurt. I think he taught me to do a lot of dangerous things. But most of all, we had fun. ☺

We used to lay on top of an old shed we had in our back yard, and Jr and his friends would shoot bb guns at the old neighbor man when he was working in his garden. They would aim for his butt when he was bent over. The bb guns must have had almost no power because he kept thinking he was getting stung by bees. Oh my, we laughed. We were naughty. But we never really hurt anyone, and we had fun.

Junior was so accident-prone. One time he and

some of the neighborhood boys made homemade spears and were spearing fish in the creek at our swimming hole. Well, one of the neighborhood boys speared Jr.'s foot. Oh my, it bled and bled.

Then one time, he was running from Mom because he was in trouble. He jumped through the basement window right onto a garden rake, and it stuck in his foot. Good grief, Jr., really?

Another accident that comes to mind is Jr. was walking across the water falls at the river and some kid through a rock. Well, it hit Jr. above his eye in the temple. Let me tell you, it was bleeding like crazy. Besides bleeding so bad, he was soaking wet from swimming, and it made it look worse. He was covered in blood by the time he walked home. Mom was hysterical. He got some stitches, and again he was fine. Sometimes I think he had nine lives like a cat. Maybe more.

I remember a boy named Dean that was my brother's and sister's friend. He was probably the best swimmer in our small town. He would dive off the pier into the water below the falls, and he was a very good swimmer. But one day, he didn't come up, and the divers from the fire station had to find him. He was trapped in an undercurrent under the falls. I was very young. But I remember how sad it made everyone in our small town. I guess Dean was a very nice person, and everyone liked him.

Jr. married the love of his life Rita when he was young. Rita and Jr. had two wonderful boys. Jerry Allan born January 9th, 1969, and Thomas Leroy born December 26th, 1969. Nothing like having them close, huh? Shortly after Jerry was born, Junior and one of his buddies decided they needed to go see the world and find themselves. Good lord. People really did that. Well, they were gone a few months. I think they did go to California and back in an old beater of a car. They would work along the way and back to have the money to move on. Rita and baby Jerry stayed with us. When Junior returned, he had not taken a bath for a while. My sister Joyce told him to go take a shower and cut his hair, or she would do it for him. He said no, but soon changed his mind when she was hauling him up the stairs to give him a shower. Remember, she was six foot one inches tall and a big woman. So, he showered, and she shaved off all his hair.

Then Junior went in the army, and he grew up. I remember when he was leaving to go to Germany, and he came to school in his uniform to tell me goodbye. I cried so hard. I think I cried not only because he was leaving, but when he walked in that school with that uniform on, for the first time in his life, he could hold his head up high. I never saw him look so handsome and so proud of who he was. It was awesome to see him be that proud. A memory that makes me cry even as I write this. We spent most of our childhood ashamed of who we were. But that day, the teachers and principal looked at my brother in his uniform in a way that they never saw him as a student, with respect. It warmed my heart to see that day.

He eventually figured life out, and he and his wife became "to me" another perfect couple. After more than twenty years together, if you saw them walking in the mall, they were holding hands. Or if you stopped over to see them and they were sitting on the couch, he would probably have his arm around her. They had those two wonderful boys, and for the most part, they were a happy family.

Brother Jr and his wife Rita on their 25th anniversary.

But on January 23, 2002, I got the call that my brother Jr. had passed away. He got up as he did every morning to drive all his grandchildren to school. His wife Rita yelled upstairs, and he said he would be right down. When she went up a few minutes later, he was on the bed and had died of a heart attack. He was fifty-two years old. It was then I realized being the youngest may not always be the greatest. And once again, I didn't get to tell him goodbye. I remember thinking, it's one thing to lose the people you love. But when it is unexpected, and you never get to say goodbye, it gets to be a bit much. There is no closure. Oh, my goodness, there was so much sadness in my heart. It hurt so bad I remember thinking, why does it have to hurt this bad? See you again one day. I miss you. Love you Jr, your sister Lola.

 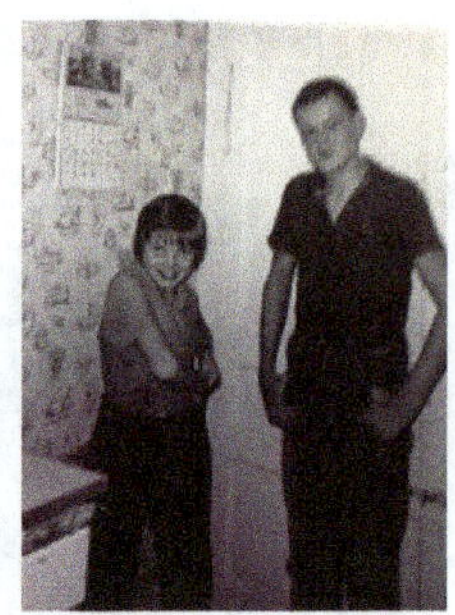

In July of 2017, my sister-in-law Rita gave me a picture that my brother put in his wallet when he left for the army. It was still there when he died over thirty years later. I know he loved me, and I loved him too. Here is that picture and a picture of my brother Elmer Jr and me a long time ago.

I miss all my family members that have left me every single day. Not in a bad way, in a good way. It would be the greatest thing to go back, even if just for one hour or one day with all of them. So sometimes, I pull a memory into my thoughts of all of us together, and it makes me smile. And sometimes, it makes me cry. And it is getting harder to recall these memories because it has been so long.

When I think of all of them being here, it is a good feeling. I have lived to see my parents, grandparents, my four brothers, a sister, a brother-in-law, three nephews, and a niece all leave this earth. YUP! Some days I feel old. But every day, I feel blessed.

On left: Left to right around 1984. My brother Bill, sister Connie, Me, my brother Gene. On right: Me with some of my siblings. Around 1988. Left to right top row: Me, Connie, Joyce. Left to right bottom: Gene and Elmer Jr.

Mom told me about her set of twin girls that were born too early, and they lived for only a couple days. She called them Mary and Michelle when she spoke of them to me. They were just too little to live in those days. And she had another son when she was home alone, and he was too little to live. She told me he was a red-headed little boy. I guess these three babies were born somewhere between 1950 and 1955. Back then, there was a place at the cemetery that was called baby land. They were all three buried there. But there were no markers for years. I assume it was a free place to put them. I went there in 2013, and there were little bricks everywhere that just said, BABE. After losing those three, she said she was done having babies.

Here are the markers that were there in 2013. Most had no names, and some just said, BABE. Not sure why they chose that spelling. But I know I have a brother and twin sisters there somewhere.

10

Me

Born Lola Jean Hewitt May 29th, 1955

Well, after my mother was done having babies, there was one more surprise. Me. The name Lola was after my father's favorite schoolteacher, and Jean was supposed to be Jane after my mother. Mom said Dad wrote it, and she always thought he spelled it wrong on purpose. I have always said I was an Oops. And Mom did always agree with me. We would laugh about it. Somehow, I do not think she was laughing at the time. She really did not want any more babies.

And boy, I guess I really upset my brother Jr.

when I was born. He didn't really like me much. Mom said every chance he got, he would steal my bottle or something just to make me cry. I think he liked it much better when he was the baby in the house.

My earliest memories are maybe when I was five or six years old. I really don't remember much before that. My memories include playing neighborhood baseball, sledding down a big hill in the street, shooting a BB gun, building tree forts, running races, homemade rafts and canoes, coal heat, and snow blowing through the window frames in our bedroom. As a kid, I don't remember ever being hugged (except by Grandma). I don't remember anyone telling me they loved me; I don't remember anyone ever tucking me into bed or reading me a book. I don't remember having books, except schoolbooks. I don't remember ever hearing the words I love you being said to anyone as a kid. I wonder why. I have no doubt my parents and siblings loved me. But no one ever said it? Maybe they did hug me, and I just don't remember? Huh. Makes me wonder sometimes. I tell my children and grandchildren I love them every time we talk, text, or see each other. And we are huggers for sure. Like I said before, my grandma was a hugger. Thank goodness she hugged me. Or I may never have known how good it felt.

Surely, I would think I had a crib when I was a baby. We had a three-bedroom house. I remember my mom had one room that was open at the top of the stairs, and you had to go through her room to get to the second bedroom. Her room also had the grate in the floor with the stove pipe going up through the roof that provided all the heat for the three bedrooms upstairs. The bedroom next to my mom's room had a set of bunk beds for my sister's two older kids, a double bed that my brother and I slept in, and one dresser. There was about one foot of space in an L shape for us to walk in that room. I slept against the wall and did not move away from that wall. My brother slept on the edge of our bed. He was embarrassed that we slept in the same bed. I imagine that was very tough for him. He was five years older than I was. I have always said, "Well, at least I always had a bed to sleep in." Unfortunately, that is more than some kids can say. I knew even then that this was a very sad truth. I didn't understand then why my brother Junior was so embarrassed, but I do now. I just thought it was great we had a bed to sleep in. And sometimes, I would sneak in and sleep with Mom. My sister Joyce had the third bedroom, and she had a crib with her baby in there. And it was the biggest bedroom. I don't remember ever having my own bed till I was thirteen or so and my mom and I moved into a little house for just the two of us. I think I must have after Junior left home. But I don't remember it.

Mom told me that she was bouncing me on the bed when I was a toddler, and I fell and literally broke the bone in my right arm at the elbow completely through. It just dangled there, I guess. They had to do surgery and put a pin in my arm for a while.  Mom said the doctor told her that I had a 50\50 chance that my arm would grow. They just really didn't know if it would grow or not. But it did. It is very crooked at the elbow, and I have a very big scar. But I am thankful every day that it grew. There my angel was again, watching over me, protecting me, and never leaving me unattended for a minute.

There must have been a plan. Now, I know my angel could not always keep me from any harm. Or I would not have had a broken arm. But I am convinced that she did push me through the toughest times in my life.

We had a water pump in the kitchen in a big sink like three feet long and maybe four inches deep. No, we did not have running water in our house. So, mom would heat water on the stove to do dishes or for baths. One day, when I was just a toddler, Mom was carrying a pan of boiling water to the sink to do dishes, and just as she came over to the sink, my brother Jr walked into the kitchen carrying me and ran into Mom and the boiling water spilled. My sister said Jr protected me and took the boiling water on his back and the back of his arms. Connie ran to Jr and pulled his t-shirt off, and she told me his skin came off with it. She said they were home from school for lunch. I cannot imagine what would have happened if the water had spilled on me. I was just a toddler. And my brother Jr. protected me. He loved me even though I disrupted him being the baby of the family. He had third-degree burns on his back and the back of his arms. Of course, he did not go to the hospital. Connie told me the doctor told Mom to put burn cream on his burns for days. And she did it faithfully. My sister Joyce told Connie Mom did it on purpose. But Connie said she did not. He was six or seven years old when this happened, and he carried those scars from this for the rest of his life. But what made it worse was it did some type of nerve damage, and his hands always shook. So, he couldn't manage a full cup of coffee. I didn't get hurt at all. There she was again. My guardian angel. She was always protecting me for some reason.

Since there was no running water in the house at all, we also didn't have a bathroom. We had an outhouse and a metal pot with a lid on it for at night when it was too cold or we just could not go outside to go for some reason. And we took a bath in the kitchen in a washtub. The big round metal tub in the middle of the kitchen was where everyone took their bath. You didn't get a lot of hot water because remember, it had to be heated in a pan on the stove. And you didn't get a bath every day. Mom would scrub us up with a washcloth between baths. And sometimes, we probably went to bed with dirt on us. I am sure it didn't hurt us in any way. Of course, we would get a bath in the kitchen sink till we were too big to fit.

We stayed busy as kids. We always played hide and go seek when we were kids. One night we were playing, and one of the boys, I think Larry, jumped in a bush to hide and came out covered in bees. It was awful. He had so many stings. I have seen what bees can do too many times. I don't like bees. I get it; they have a purpose. But I still don't like them. We swam in the river, built tree forts, made mud pies, squished our toes in the mud, played in the rain, climbed trees, played hide and go seek, rode our bicycles everywhere, and truly lived a life all kids should get to live. We were kids that had fun, and it cost no money whatsoever. I remember climbing trees catching salamanders and frogs. I was very good at catching nightcrawlers. It was nothing to catch ten or twelve dozen in one night. And we sold them for 25¢ a dozen. We were rich if we had two dollars. We used to get salamanders in our yard every year for a week or two. Lots of them. It was so much fun to catch them. They would be all over the yard at night.

There were a couple good hills to go sledding on too. But we also would go to the top of the hill in front of our house and sled down the road for a couple blocks. And we would build a snow fort out of the whole front yard. I doubt kids do that any-more. They have no idea what they are missing. In the summer, we were barefoot, and I loved to run. I would race almost anyone down the full block in front of our house, and I had to be barefoot. I could not run very well with shoes on. The highway and main street through our town were blacktop. But the roads in town and in front of my house were gravel. I still loved to run, and I was fast. I could beat a lot of people. I used to think I was fast because I would count to myself when I ran. The faster I counted, the faster I ran. It made sense to me. I never told anyone that till right now. I guess I thought that is what everyone did. And maybe they do.

There was a dream I had over and over when I was little. I think maybe as often as once a week or more. Maybe everyone has this dream as a kid. I could fly. It became so real in my mind. I would just wave my arms, and up I would go. I would be up by the tops of the trees, looking at everyone in my yard. They never understood how I did it. They would ask me how I did it, and I would show them. But no matter how hard they tried, no one else could fly. When I was up there, no one could get me. I am not sure who I was getting away from. But I felt safe up there. Maybe my angel took me there sometimes so I would not be afraid. Now that is a very nice thought.

Today, I don't really like heights, but I do wish I could fly like in those dreams. It was so wonderful and gave me a real sense of freedom and protection. If you can fly, no person or animal could ever hurt you except a bird or a bee. And I am not afraid of birds.

I also loved being in the river, and I was many times long before I could swim. My brothers and sisters would throw me in a tube and tell me to hang on. Then they would go do their own thing. I remember one time, in my inner tube, I came face to face with a water moccasin. It scared the living daylight out of me. I think I walked on water. Either that or the screeching I did scared it to death. It really was so much fun, though. Oh, and sometimes I would play with dolls with other little girls. I was playing dolls one time with my friend down the street on her porch. A mud wasp landed on my hand, and she told me to keep very still. So, I did, and the wasp stung me. I was really upset. From then on, if there was any kind of bee, I did not hold still. I would run or try to kill it. But for the most part, I didn't play dolls much because I was a tomboy.

Once we were school age, the school had a program where we could take a school bus to Charles City, twenty miles away, and get swimming lessons in the summer. It was a free school program. After all, we lived in a town with a river going through it, and we did not have a pool in our town. But if we wanted to swim after lessons, it was a quarter for pleasure swimming. Sometimes we had a quarter, and sometimes we did not. So, we had to wait outside the fence while the other kids swam. And sometimes, we would have a nickel for laughy taffy. That was a great treat! I so looked forward to this every summer. Does life get any better as a kid than a bus ride with all your friends twenty miles to a swimming pool, swimming lessons, a quarter for pleasure swimming, and to have a nickel for Laffy taffy? Life could not ever get any better than that. Not when I was a kid anyway.

One of my not-so-pleasant memories, when I was little, is I was jumping on the couch like a trampoline, throwing a fit, no doubt, and I fell. I hit the edge of the windowsill and shoved my front top tooth up under my nose. I was bleeding and scream-ing. Mom grabbed me and ran all the way across town to take me to the dentist to have it pulled out. It was at least ten or twelve blocks away. I can't even imagine what people thought when they saw my mom running carrying a screaming kid all the way across town. We didn't have a telephone most of the time when I was a kid. We had a car. But of course, Dad would have had it at work. And Mom didn't drive. We walked everywhere. We walked to the gro-cery store, the doctor, to school, to play with our friends across town, everywhere. We would walk to the grocery store and carry all our groceries home. It was about eight blocks.

Every single Halloween, my sister Joyce would take my brother Junior and me to every house in town that we could possibly get to in one night. We would have more candy on Halloween than we had all the rest of the year. We must have walked ten miles on Halloween night. Boy, was that candy a treat for us. But of course, my sister Joyce would take her share. She had a sweet tooth, and she would soon have diabetes very bad.

At Christmas time, every classroom in school would have a real Christmas tree. On the last day of school before Christmas break, they would let someone that needed a tree bring it home. Sometimes we would get to bring it home. I don't remember how we would get a tree if we didn't get it from school. Maybe we always did get one from school. I would be so excited. We were going to have a Christmas tree. We would string popcorn and decorate the tree. I am sure the only decorations we had were handmade. I don't remember ever having lights on our tree. I am not sure we ever did. The best part of Christmas when I was a kid was Mom, and my sisters would make a lot of cookies. I remember the whole table being covered with frosted cookies. And Mom would make homemade fruit cake. I never understood fruitcake. In my opinion, it is not anything that belongs in the cake family. It is gross. We would have oyster stew and oyster crackers sometimes on Christmas eve. The *only* thing good about oyster stew is the little round oyster crackers. But

I would have the juice from the stew with some oyster crackers. Remember, if you didn't eat what was on the table, there was not something else to eat. I did not eat those oysters. I remember thinking, "Who on earth thought of eating such a thing as an oyster?" "And what the heck is it anyway?" It made no sense to me. I called it eyeball stew. Sometimes we would get a present for Christmas. But sometimes, we just got candy, fruit, and nuts. One year all I wanted was a record player. But I got a pair of pajamas instead. I remember they were too big, and they had polka dots on them. I am sure they were on sale somewhere. I think I got a record player later when Mom could afford it. One year I got a pair of ice skates. They were about three sizes too big. But I wore them anyway. Again, I am sure they were on sale, or Mom thought she would give me plenty of room to grow.

Looking back at my first job, I worked in the cafeteria at school. I remember I made about $11.00 a month, and one Christmas, I think I gave everyone in my family a present. I remember I bought my mom some powder that smelled like lilacs. That was a great fragrance back then. And lilac bushes do smell beautiful. Giving everyone in my family a present was like getting the greatest gift I could possibly get. I still, to this day, love to give gifts. Thus, I will forever be poor.

Have you ever heard the story from your parents that they walked a mile to school and back every day, uphill both ways, in the worst of blizzards? I must have been about six or seven years old, and we walked four blocks to school, and it was not uphill. That was easy. But there was a blizzard, and I didn't own any long pants or snow pants. Girls wore dresses, and pants were not something we always had the luxury of having. Well, I got about 3½ blocks, and I laid down in the snow because I just couldn't walk any longer. My legs were frozen. I was crying, and I just could not keep walking. I could show you today exactly where I laid down in the snow. Thank goodness, I walked with the neighbor girl that day. She tugged and tugged on me to get up, and she helped me get the rest of the way. If she hadn't been there, I am not sure what would have happened. Oh my, I would not be here if I did not have someone watching over me every minute of every day. I do wonder how my mother could have let me out the door in a freezing blizzard to walk to school with bare legs. Was she there? Did she know? I'm not sure. Need I say who else was there? My Angel.

She just never left me for even a minute. Sometimes I had long pants to wear under my dress. But when I didn't, my legs were always beat red when I got to school and beat red when I got home in the winter. Most kids walked to school, and that was just the way it was. Very few families had more than one car back then. I don't remember anyone who did.

I remember one time in grade school, a girl told me her mom said she couldn't play with me because I had a bad family, and we were poor. I think I cried. I didn't understand what that had to do with me. But I remember it made me feel ashamed of myself and of my family for the very first time. To be ashamed of your family and yourself is the absolute worst feeling as a kid. You can erase a lot in life. But shame is the worst emotion in the world to try to erase. It truly is. It just can't be taken away.

I was a skinny kid and grew up quick. I knew how to wash clothes in the wringer washer by the time I was ten or twelve years old or if I needed one thing washed, I washed it in the sink by hand and hung it on the clothesline to dry, even in the winter. We never owned a dryer. I would hang them on the line outside or in the basement. We would hang them outside sometimes in the winter, then bring them in and hang them in the basement. There would be six lines or so, the full length of the basement full of clothes hanging to dry. And sometimes, I would put them on the heater in the living room to dry and watch them very close and turn them over, so they would not burn. I scorched and ruined more than one thing drying it on the heater. And remember, we did not have running water. So, we filled the wringer washer and rinse tubs with a bucket, and dropped the hose out the back door to drain them. I knew how to sew by hand by the time I was ten and could hand sew a zipper in a pair of pants. I could darn socks perfectly. It was like an art. You just put a lightbulb in the sock and sew back and forth a lot till there is a patch on the sock. I am sure that is a lost art for sure. Now we just throw them away and buy new ones.

When there is no one there to do things for you, you simply learned to do them yourself. Oh, my mom did laundry, and she did sew. She just wasn't always available to do these things when you needed them done.

The clothesline outside had a dual purpose. In the summer, we would put a blanket over one line and pull the corners out as far as we could and pound a clothespin in each corner for a tent. It worked great! I would venture to guess we ruined the corners of most of the blankets in our house. It was so fun. And we would curl up in a blanket and sleep in that tent overnight. It was so peaceful. Even though we ruined the corners of the blankets, they still worked just fine for a blanket on our beds.

My mom was a short, red-headed, hot-headed Irish woman. She had a temper. If you mouthed off, she would slap your mouth. And it hurt. I did something once that showed me just how bad it could get. I'm not sure what I did. Maybe I didn't quite tell the truth or talked disrespectful to her. I can't remember. I was a mouthy teenager, just like most are. I remember feeling angry at my mother most of the time when I was a teenager. I am not sure why she would get so angry. Maybe because she was trapped with so many babies to care for. I think this made her angry. Anyway, this one time, she beat me with a belt until my sister Joyce took the belt away from her. If Joyce had not taken it, I do believe she would have beat me till I was bleeding or worse. I absolutely refused to cry. If I would have cried, I think she would have stopped. But I would not cry because I wanted to hurt her like she hurt me. I had welts all over my body. They were on my arms, legs, back, stomach; absolutely everywhere. The only one I could not cover up when I went to school was on my neck. I told the school that I fell and hit something, of course. I am sure they knew what a welt from a beating with a belt looked like. That was the one, and only time she ever did that. I wonder now why my family didn't have social services at our house all the time?

When I was thirteen, some new neighbors moved in a couple blocks down the road. One of the boys liked me and gave me a pearl ring that had both a white pearl and a black pearl. But we were young, and it didn't last long. Then his family moved away. But he still always liked me. Little did I know he would someday be the father to two of my children?

Around this time, all the kids went to the local

café after school and had a coke and french fries. That place was packed every day. It was so fun. By this time, I had settled in with a group of kids that were the cool kids. Some had money, and some were poor. *But we were all **cool.*** I felt like I fit in, and I had finally found a place to belong. A place to belong is so important to a teenager. I have wondered when I hear of a teenager that commits suicide today... Did they not find a place to fit in and belong? It is so important. We all need that place during those years. Even if it's the wrong place.

So, I was then part of the cool group in school. But being part of the cool gang came with a price. We smoked, we drank beer at parties, and we were wild teenagers. But we were cool, and that is what mattered. I had a place to belong, and they cared about me, right? We had parties every weekend at the forest preserve north of town. We were partiers for sure. Now, I was somewhat mature physically when I was young, so of course, the boys like that. I only really had two boyfriends during these years. They had three things in common. They were cool, they really liked me, and they were not poor like I was. They both lived in nice houses, wore nice clothes, and had material things in life that they *wanted*. They both made me feel so special that they wanted me to be their girlfriend.

My girlfriends and I would take the bus to the next town Mason City on Saturday, where there was plenty of shopping etc. It cost 50 cents each way. I had two girlfriends that would shoplift. So, to be cool, I had to try it. I went to Ben Franklin and stole a little thing of blue eye shadow. It would have cost maybe twenty-nine cents or something. All the way home on the bus, I was sure someone saw me and that I was going to jail. Or worse yet, my mom would find out and beat me within an inch of my life. OMG!! I was so scared. That was my career as a thief. I never had the nerve to do it again. Besides that, it was wrong. I learned right from wrong at a very early age in my life. We never got a time out if we were naughty. We got hit hard enough to remember we did not want to be hit again. And we learned right from wrong when we did something once for sure. I now know that was not always a bad thing. There are kids today that could benefit from this behavior.

My family was more dysfunctional and violent that most kids ever need to be around. But, for some reason, I managed to build survival skills that would get me through life. There were a couple times I almost gave up on this journey. But all in all, my journey has been far from boring. I have been extremely fortunate to experience life. I figure some people just go through life and never really experience living. That was not the case for me. I have lived through extreme sadness, unbelievable happiness, being very poor, to being comfortable in life, being ashamed of who I was and of my family, to being very proud of myself and of my family. As I said before, you don't get to pick your family, but you do get to pick how you see them with your heart. It is your choice. Open your heart or close it. I am pretty sure my heart has never learned to close. It is open to pretty much everyone and everything. I am not sure how big it is. But it is never too full for just one more person. Sometimes that is good and sometimes not so much. There have been people that have taken advantage of my big heart in my life more than once.

When I look back, I have known my angel was there so many times in my life. I have no other explanation for how circumstances that could have been so bad, even in my adult life, somehow turned out ok at the last minute. Luck? I don't really think so.

Somehow, I have chosen the right path that would get me through the toughest of times. I look back sometimes and think, every time I would get to a tough spot in life, feel like I was on the edge of a cliff, or want to give up, she was always behind me, pushing me forward for all she was worth. I have no other explanation.

Which makes me ask this. "What have I done, or what am I supposed to do in my life to deserve all that I have been given?" I ask Mom, I ask Dad, I ask God. What am I supposed to do now? I stood in church one day and asked God, 'Why am I lost"? Mom, Dad, God, will one of you show me what I am supposed to do now? I am now sixty-two years old and feel like there is still something I am supposed to do. I just wish someone would let me know what it is. Maybe, write this book? I really don't know. Do other people feel this way? I have never met anyone else that does. And maybe some people do, and they just don't talk about it. So, I guess I will keep doing what I am doing and hopefully make a difference somewhere along the way. That is what I do hope for. To make a difference in someone's life. Or many people's lives. I hope I already have somewhere along the way. I like to think that I have. It makes me smile.

But most of all, since the earliest memories of my life, I felt different from anyone else that ever came into my life. My family, my friends, everyone. I always wondered why people did what they did, why there were mean people in the world, why some people get sick and die so young, why don't we all just have a certain number of years to live, and we know what that is, why some people had so much money and material things, and some had so little, why was I born into a poor family, why, why, why? My dad worked very hard, but they drank and gambled. I guess my mom much more than my dad. I get that part. But why didn't someone stop them, so maybe we could have had a different life?

11

∽

My Mom and Dad

Elmer L. Hewitt born, Born August 18, 1916

Betty J. Lewis born, June 14, 1925

I was teased when I was a kid because we were poor, because my brother was in prison, because of my gay brother\Uncle, because my sister had three kids and was never married, and oh, as I have mentioned, my parents drank....... often. My dad worked hard Monday thru Friday at the lumber yard. He and my mom would go to the bar, not every night, but most nights. They drank beer and played cards for money. They had big round tables in the bar just for gambling. Now, do you think that drinking and gambling may have been some of the reason we were so poor? I am pretty sure it was. Because my dad always worked. Oh, my parents wouldn't stay at the bar as late during the week as they did on weekends. But if you wanted to see either of them most nights, you had to go to the bar and for sure on Friday and Saturday night. The Friday and Saturday schedule in our house was.... Mom and Dad went to the bar and drank. Most weeks, my parents would come home at least one night and fight. We would lay in bed terrified. I remember one time my brother Jr. and I ran to the neighbors and had them call the police because they were fighting so bad. Remember, we didn't have a telephone most of the time. The neighbors that had a phone were Vivian and Harry. I remember them like it was yesterday. Vivian used to make these huge crispy cookies with cinnamon and sugar on them, and she would give us one sometimes. Oh my!! They were so good. Unfortunately, Harry was one of the people that was always suspected of poisoning our dogs. Anyway, the police would come and take my dad to jail. I remember this particular time that I stood in the front yard and cried when they took him. I didn't want my parents to fight. But I didn't want the police to take my dad either. He spent the night in jail, and they brought him home in the morning. I don't remember if we did this many times or how often the police came. I always heard my brother Jerry left when he was sixteen years old because he could not take the fighting. I was six years old when Jerry left, and we already know my sister Connie left when she was thirteen because of the fighting.

So, I must believe the fighting was much worse than I remember.

Sometimes on Sunday, my parents would haul us kids to their friends, and there would be three or four couples and everyone's kids. They would have beer already, or someone would go to Minnesota and buy it. The adults would drink themselves stupid, and all the kids would run wild. The boys sometimes drove the cars in the fields, and the parents didn't even know. That is just how it was. I learned over the years that it really was my mom that caused most of the problems. That is very hard for me because my dad divorced my mom for another woman when I was very young. I remember Dad came to visit me sometimes on weekends. One time he brought me a big bag of orange slices. They were these gooey orange-flavored candies with sugar on the outside. I ate the whole bag. I was not feeling too well after that, and I really got sick. My dad really was a nice man. He was my dad, and I loved him.

And my dad wasn't really a mean man, and I don't think that my parents would fight so much when they weren't drinking. I remember Dad bought us kids cane poles, and Mom, Dad, and us kids had a picnic by the river and fished with our very own fishing poles. It was awesome! What a great memory of a real happy family. I wish there were more of these memories. But I only remember this one time. And my mother helped me remember this one. I had it tucked away somewhere, never to be found.

I can remember my mom wore an apron every day. She did not drive a car, and I do not think many moms did. Moms stayed home and sometimes worked at home. And Dads went to work. My mother ironed to make money. She would wash white shirts for businessmen hang them on the line to dry, then sprinkle them with water and starch and fold them and roll them tight. Each shirt was about six inches long and a couple inches around when they were prepared to iron. I don't know where she would get all these shirts. Maybe from the cleaners? I am sure she did not make a lot of money doing this, and it was a terrific amount of work. They were always all white, and I think sometimes she would have thirty or forty shirts. When she had them all rolled in the basket, she would start to iron. She would iron for hours. And she would sing. My mother had a beautiful voice. I loved to hear her sing. When it is quiet at night, and I recall a memory of her singing, I can still hear her. But it is getting harder to hear the older I get. She loved country music and would sometimes play a record when she sang. It is one of my most fond memories as a child. Singing is a sign of happiness, you know. So, I like to think singing made her happy.

One of the other neighbor ladies baked for the local bakery. She was an Indian woman and had four boys. She would make dozens of cinnamon rolls at night and put them in the refrigerator. Then get up real early in the morning and bake them. We would get to have one sometimes. They were so delicious.

Mom always said, "Don't sweep off your neighbor's doorstep till you have swept off your own." I used to think, "what the heck does that mean?" I now know. "Don't judge another person till you judge yourself." She had lots of weird sayings. But they all meant something. And most of them I will never forget.

We grew a garden bigger than many people's yards are today. And Mom would can vegetables like crazy. She canned green beans, corn, tomatoes, pickles, and beets. I did not like the smell of beets being canned in the house. And the house would smell like beets for days. And we always had a huge bin in the basement for potatoes all winter. Somehow, we always had canned peaches. I am not sure where my mom got the peaches. Peddlers would sometimes come around selling stuff. I think maybe that is where she got them.

This was the lot where we had our garden, and it is still there today. See those lilac bushes on the right? Our house is on the left.

On birthdays, we would sometimes have homemade ice cream. But I only remember having it in the winter because we needed snow to make it. And we would all take turns turning the handle till it was ready. It seemed to take forever. Sometimes Mom would put peaches or strawberries in it. Oh my gosh, it was so good.

One day I came home from school, and there was a lady in our house with red hair, pink cheeks, and ruby red lips. I must have been eight or nine years old. This woman grabbed my cheeks and said, "Lola Jean, look how big you are!" She was scary-looking with all that makeup on. It was my real Grandma (Mom's Mother). I always heard the stories how she was a gypsy and traveled around with bands and played the harmonica and accordion. That was the first time I remember ever seeing her. And she was nothing like my grandma. She was scary. She finally settled in California with someone that made her happy, and they married. I saw her one other time when I was thirteen. I went to California in the car with my mom and Uncle Ike, and Aunt Lois. My grandma was having a pacemaker put in her heart. So, we went to Englewood, Ca. for her surgery. She was in surgery for many hours. But the night before she went in the hospital, she played her accordion and harmonica for us, and she gave me a diamond ring that I later gave to my daughter for her sixteenth birthday. We really had a nice visit. That was the second time I ever saw her and the last time.

My mother didn't start driving till I was a teenager. After Dad died, Grandpa would take Mom to the city like once a month to get whatever she needed for groceries, etc. I remember if we got to go along, we had to sit with our feet on the mat on the floor (if they reached). Grandpa would forbid us to put our feet on the back of the front seat or under it. And we had to sit still, or we could not go. My grandpa was so strict.

I am sure we ate what we had access to. Mom made salmon patties from salmon in a can. They were disgusting. She put eggs and crackers in it and mixed it all up, made them into patties, and fried them like a hamburger. There were these round bones in them, and you would have to make sure you didn't eat them. Bean soup, cornbread, pea and potato soup, and creamed peas on toast were regulars around my house. Mom would put milk and butter in the peas and thicken them with a little flour. Then you pour it over toast. **Voila!! Shit on shingles.** It was very good and filling. I made it for my children when they were young too. I eventually made chipped beef on toast. I remember later in life, I ordered creamed peas on toast in Missouri at a restaurant. I was shocked to see they had it. And they called it what we did. But on the menu, it was called creamed peas on toast. The two things we ate too much of was bean soup and cornbread. I swore that when I was grown and bought my own groceries, I was not going to eat bean soup or cornbread ever again. And I didn't for years. But I will now.

We never really had much meat unless my brothers shot it or caught it. We ate rabbit, squirrel, pheasant, and river fish. We didn't have a lot. But for the most part, I don't remember that we ever really went hungry. We were skinny, but I think we were healthy. Except I was always anemic as a kid and had to take these huge iron pills that made me sick to my stomach. They were awful.

Homemade bread was something we always had. My mom made the best fresh bread in the world once a week. I remember she made like ten loaves or something every week. On bread baking day, dinner was awesome! Mom would save some bread dough for fritters. She would pull hunks of bread dough and drop them in a pan of hot lard till they were golden brown. We would put butter and syrup or sugar on them. OMG! If you haven't had these, you haven't lived. They were the best. Our syrup was sugar and water boiled on the stove. I thought that was syrup and made it for my own kids for years. I learned to add maple flavoring, and eventually, I learned to buy the syrup in the store. But I still prefer my syrup to be hot even to this day. It must be hot. For many years if I closed my eyes and really thought about it, I could smell that fresh bread right out of the oven. That must be one of the best smells in the world. This memory is getting harder to recall as I get older. And the smell is gone.

When I was in grade school, we had a dog named Blacky, and he would come to the school to meet us and walk home with us every day. He always waited across the street from the school. We never trained him to do that. He was just very smart and missed us when we were away. We had to ride the bus to school in another town Rock Falls, Ia., for third and fourth grade only. One day I was riding the bus back from Rock Falls after school, and the bus swerved and almost went in the ditch about a block from the school where we turned. He swerved and killed our dog. I saw it out the bus window. The bus driver did it on purpose just to be mean. My dog never hurt anyone. He knew I was on that bus, and he was excited. I have always wondered why some people are just mean. And why on earth do I need to know them? I cried and cried. Blacky would no longer be waiting for us after school. How much pain can one's little heart take when just a child? I really don't know. But I tend to think I had more than my fair share of heartache as a child. And I sometimes wonder if that bus driver got to go to heaven. Would God forgive him for killing such a great companion for these kids that needed him so much? I don't know. Maybe.

Unfortunately, I also realized at a young age that my dad was sick. He had ulcerative colitis. When he got too sick to work and he was going to die, the other woman that he left my mom for left him. He went in the hospital to die when I was eight years old. Drinking and ulcerative colitis don't go well together. But he drank anyway, and I am sure it contributed to his death. Did he know he was doing that? I don't know. The rules at the hospital were you had to be twelve years old to go in and visit someone. So, everyone got to go see my dad in the hospital when he was there to die except me. They got to talk to him and tell him what he meant to them. A few hours before my dad died, they let me come in to say goodbye. He was in a coma by then. But Mom had me sit next to him and hold his hand. She said I needed to talk to him and that he knew I was there and could hear me, but he couldn't talk back. He must have weighed under a hundred pounds, and he was over six feet tall. I sat right there and talked and watched my dad stop breathing. When that happened, Mom took me out of the room, and the nurses went in there. He was gone, and I didn't get to give him a hug or hear him say he loved me. I didn't get to hear him say he was proud of me or that he would miss me. I didn't get to tell him not to leave or that I loved him. I didn't get to ask him to stay. I didn't get to say goodbye. I was eight years old, and on 7/31/1963, my dad died. I was so sad. And my heart broke beyond belief. I remember I could feel it physically hurt. Even though he was angry sometimes, I didn't want him to leave me. I wish he could have been around to watch me grow up. I wish he had known my children and my grandchildren. I wish he hadn't been sick and that life had been a little better to him. I still talk to him sometimes, and I miss him so much every day. I think my heart almost died on that day.

If I won the lottery tomorrow, I would be more

excited about what I could do for other people than myself. I always thought the first thing I would do was get a big comfortable car and go get my sisters and take them shopping. They would get all new clothes. Then I would get them each a house next to each other. They live too far apart. I would take care of them. I could not give them money because they would give it all away and not take care of themselves just as they do now. Neither of them is in good health. New clothes are something they don't ever need. They always know someone else that needs something much more than they do.

They have both worked so hard all their life. But everything they ever had they gave away to someone else. They gave of themselves till it wore them out. My sister Joyce raised her three kids, her husband's four kids, two granddaughters, a grandson, and she was trying to raise a great-grandson when she had to lose her leg. She was told she could no longer have him. It broke her heart. She cried and cried. So, she found his dad, that he never knew, and he wanted him. He has a wonderful home now and came to see her all the time while she was alive. It really was a good thing.

Well, I have been writing for over four years and

have now lost my sister Joyce on 3/23/2015. So, the dream of taking care of them both while they lived close to one another is not ever going to happen. It really is sad.

I do believe all this loss has interfered with my relationships with people. I remember for years thinking if I loved someone, they would leave me. I did get over that some with my kids. But I have always had a demon that keeps me awake at night worrying about losing those I love. It is a demon I have learned to live with to this day. It is what it is, and I don't think I will ever be rid of it.

In 2018 I decided to go to grief counseling. I was pretty sure losing my mother was the single worst loss of my life. But to my surprise, it was my dad. Being eight years old and watching him die left me with a lot of pain. During this counseling, I went through quite a different exercise that gave me some peace with my father's death. I had to close my eyes and tell the whole story of when he died twice. Then I closed my eyes and told the whole story and rewrote it. When I told it this time, he was awake when I went to the hospital; he hugged me and told me how much he loved me, how proud of me he was, and that he would miss me terrible. I told him how much I loved him and that I did not want him to go because I would miss him so much. It was a good feeling rewriting this end of life and imagining how it would have been if the hospital rules had not robbed me of telling my dad goodbye and that I loved him. It truly was a good experience. It really is quite ok if I want my memory of losing my dad to be the story I rewrote. I am sure he would not mind at all.

So, with that said:

In the order that I lost you,

Elmer Leroy Sr. "My Dad" 1963, I was eight years old.

Jerry Allen "Jerry, my brother" 1967, I was twelve years old.

Arthur Maxwell "my grandpa" 1971, I was sixteen years old.

Verna Mae "biological grandmother"1972, I was seventeen years old.

Betty Jane "my mother" 1984, I was twenty-nine years old.

Marie Elizabeth "my grandma" 1986 I was thirty-one years old.

Scott David "Joyce's son, my nephew" 1992, I was thirty-seven years old.

Elmer Leroy Jr. "Junior, my brother" 2002, I was forty-seven years old.

William Perry "Bill, my brother" 2003, I was forty-eight years old.

Eugene Arthur "Gene, my brother" 2008, I was fifty-two years old.

Thomas Leroy "Junior's son, my nephew" 2009, I was fifty-three years old.

Joyce Allice "Joyce, my sister" 2015, I was sixty years old.

William Leroy "Connie's son, my nephew" 2015, I was sixty years old.

Tracy Lynn "Jerry's Daughter, my niece" 2016, I was sixty-one years old.

"It is time for me to say goodbye" and tell all of you I still love you and how very much I miss you every day. I truly hope you are all together and that you have found a way to forgive one another for all the pain that was endured because some of you lost your way in life or because your life was just too hard to bear. I will see you again one day. And I hope you look down on all of us with pride and smile.

Thanks again Mom.

12

∾

My life continues with great sadness.

Looking back, my first love as a teenager, we were just very different. He took me shopping and bought me nice clothes. He had me to his house, and his family was very nice to me. But he was a troubled teenager, and he was not content to be in a relationship with me. So, he broke my heart. And once again, I felt that maybe I didn't deserve someone like him. After all, my family was poor, and we were not as good as families like his. I will admit, though, you never really forget your first love, be it good or bad. Unfortunately, he would return one day.

Then there was someone that I had a very different relationship with. We made each other smile. When he hugged me, I felt like the world was a better place. We partied with our friends and had so much fun. And he was very protective of me. A previous boyfriend said something mean to me at a party once, and he beat him up bad. I guess maybe that made me feel loved? I am not sure, but we were a very happy couple. He was two years older than me. He was seventeen, and I was fifteen. During our relationship, he got in a car accident and broke his jaw in several places and knocked out all his front teeth. His mom called my mom and said he wanted me at the hospital. I am sure his mom did not want to call. Because their family had a completely different social status than my family did. But she did, and my mom took me there to see him and sit with him. I do believe to this day that he loved me. And I loved him. I still believe we had the real kind of love. If I saw him, my stomach would probably get butterflies to this day. It is now in 2021, and this has proven to be wrong.

Not too long after his accident, we broke up. I

don't remember why. I didn't have a new boyfriend, and I suddenly was getting sick. My doctor did some tests, and I tested positive for diabetes. So, I was put in the hospital for a few days to get it under control. I was put in a room with a black woman named Lola. Now, what are the chances of that? I had never even spoken to a black person before. And she was the first Lola I had ever met. She was a wonderful person. But every time the phone on the nightstand between us rang, the wrong Lola would answer. After three days or so, I got out of the hospital and went right back to eating ice cream and drinking beer with my friends. At fifteen years old, you are invincible, right?

Little did anyone know (including me) that I was pregnant, and that is why my blood sugar was out of control. Within a few weeks, this became a reality. I was going to have a baby. Of course, my mother was not pleased. And I had no idea how far along I was. So, mom tried a couple home remedies to make me miscarry the baby, and they didn't work. I was too far along. So, I was fifteen years old and going to have a baby. At first, the father of my baby and I didn't talk. We were both very upset. Now, how stupid is that? We were surprised. Really? Then, one night we got together and went to my mother's, and he asked her if he could marry me. She said yes. I was so excited. So, he left and went home to tell his parents that we were getting married. He told me that he loved me and everything was going to be all right. After that night, he never talked to me ever again. We have not seen each other or spoken one word since that night. You see, he was from a prominent family. Like it or not, they had money, and we did not. I lived on the wrong side of the railroad tracks to marry their son. I have often wondered if his parents were ever sorry for what they did. I now know it turned out the way it should have. Like I said before, I think he really did love me. But at the time, my heart ached beyond belief. I was so afraid and so alone for many months to come. There was this little baby inside of me, and I had nothing to offer it but heartache and sorrow. The sadness I felt was beyond belief. I was so scared.

Sometime early during my pregnancy, my mom bought me a magazine. On the cover was a headline that read "Babies having Babies" I read it, and it basically gave some very clear and real facts about life with a new baby. Up during the night, no hanging out with friends, can't go to school. And it explained that you are responsible for this new little baby and the life they would have. I was done with school anyway. You weren't really allowed in school when you were pregnant back then. Reality was I had nothing to give this new little baby that deserved everything the world had to offer. Things I could never give it at fifteen years old. So, I made the single hardest decision I would ever make in my life. I decided to give my baby up for adoption to someone that couldn't have a baby. I convinced myself that it was the right thing to do. And I would sometimes imagine how happy this couple, I never knew, would be when their new baby came to share its life as their child.

So now, here I was, homeless and not welcome at my stepdad's house. I stayed with each of my sisters sometimes. But mostly I stayed with friends. I had a friend that had her own apartment and would let me stay with her and sleep on her couch. She would take me to her parent's house to eat sometimes, and they were very nice to me. She came from a big family, and I was just another kid. Nice is an important thing to me. I really did have people in my life during this time who just happened to be sincerely nice people. I absolutely do not want anything to do with people that are not genuinely nice. I still hung out with all my friends and went to parties. But I didn't drink anymore. And I didn't have a boyfriend. I cannot count how many nights I cried myself to sleep alone on someone's couch. I never saw the father of my baby anymore. I think sometimes my friends made sure they had me doing things that would not put him and me in the same place. Little did I know, he was gone.

I had a male friend that was a few years older than me, and we hung out a lot. He may have been older, but he was so good to me. He was one of those genuinely nice people. He would let me drive his car around until I couldn't fit behind the steering wheel and reach the foot pedal. And I didn't have a license. He drove a sporty car. I think maybe it was a Barracuda. He was just an all-around nice guy. He said once that he could marry me, and he would help me, so I could keep my baby. I said no, that wouldn't be right. We were just friends. But he was a great guy. I often wonder where he is. So, life just kind of went on, and I stayed wherever until it was almost time for my baby to be born.

When it was almost time to have my baby, I went to stay with Mom. I am sure the only reason I got to go to her house was because she was still legally re-sponsible for me. I was about to endure something that no one prepared me at fifteen years of age to go through. I didn't get any pain medicine or any-thing. And there was a nurse that was mean to me. She would tell me to shut up and quit screaming. She would tell me it didn't really hurt that bad and that I needed to quit carrying on so. I finally asked her if she had any kids, and she said no. After that, I had some not-so-nice things to say to her, and she backed off a little. But I kept getting out of bed and going to the bathroom, thinking I had to go. So, they put the rails up and said I had to stay in bed. I am not sure how you prepare for giving birth when you are fifteen. No one prepared me at all. There were no classes or coaches. I knew nothing except that it was going to be painful. I had no idea what was going to happen. During this time, I really was sure I was going to die. I was scared to death. The pain was so bad I remember getting somewhat delirious. I had no idea what was going on. And no one told me anything, even during the event. After twenty hours or so, on January 26th, 1971, the nurse wheeled me in a room to give birth. They put a sheet up, so I couldn't see what was going on, and I gave birth to my baby that I would never see. I could have seen my baby. But I knew if I did, I might not do what was best for my baby. So, I chose not to see or hold my child, and I was moved to another floor in the hospital immediately after giving birth. That was my choice. My heart would have begged me to do otherwise. And it may have won. I was so sad. When would the sadness in my life ever end?

I was in a room all by myself, and Mom went home till I was released from the hospital three or four days later. I was there alone, and I think the only visitor I had once was my sister Connie came to see me. I don't remember. I blocked so much of this time in my life out of my memory. It is really hidden in a place in my memory bank that I struggle to recall. I don't remember spending much time with my baby's father. I don't remember the pain, giving birth, or so many things. It is so hard to explain. I know these things happened, but the live memories are not there. They are really buried somewhere. I think that is a coping mechanism that some of us learn at an early age. We can take some of the most painful things in the memory bank and build a huge wall around them so they cannot resurface. This must be what I have done with most of these memories. Because at sixty-five (fifty years later), I can remember so many memories about my life like it was yesterday. But this period of my life is mostly facts that I know and very few realistic memories. It is kind of like a dream that you remember a few parts, but not the whole dream. Giving up my baby was like sticking a knife in my heart for a long time. That I do remember.

The adoption was done through a private attorney, and the people that adopted my baby paid for all my medical care. Like I said, as soon as the baby was born, I was taken to a different floor in the hospital. When the attorney came the next day with the papers, he put a sheet of paper over the names of the people that would be my baby's new parents. He told me I could remove it and see their names if I wanted to. I chose not to. I thought that was for the best. I have truly never had one day that I thought I did the wrong thing and have always been ok with my decision. At fifteen, I remember thinking I should be proud that even though I made a mistake in life, the result was going to be that someone that couldn't have a baby was going to get one. I could only imagine how excited they would be. I would try to visualize them when they had that beautiful baby put in their arms for the first time. That really gave me some peace. Because the pain in my heart was so bad, I thought I would die. If this was the best for my baby, why did my heart hurt so bad? At that time, I think my heart almost turned to stone. I really wasn't sure what was in store for my life.

There was a rumor that my baby's father went around passing out cigars when he heard I gave birth. I never really knew if that was true. I now know that this was not true. He was far away.

I did go back to my mom's for just a couple days when I was released from the hospital. But I wasn't really wanted there. So, she was driving me to my sister's house, and we came over a hill in the country, and there were about 20 feeder pigs in the road. Mom could not stop fast enough, and we hit them. I was in so much pain. We sat in the farmer's house till someone came to get us because the car was not drivable. So, at fifteen years old, I was still homeless and just stayed wherever I hadn't worn out my welcome. Mom married my stepdad, and I didn't fit in there. I wasn't part of their plan.

Adoptions were not final for a year back then. I called the attorney about a year later to see if everything was on track to be finalized, and he assured me it was. No one knew I called. I went to a payphone to make the call. I was sick to my stomach that day. I always believed I did what was best for my baby. But it physically hurt in my heart terrible. I heard rumors in the family that Mom looked through the window when I gave birth and told everyone I had a boy. But I tried not to listen to anything anyone said.

About a month after giving up my baby, I was staying at my sister's for a couple days, and an old boyfriend came around. He was the one that had given me the pearl ring when I was thirteen. He still wanted me to be his girlfriend. So, I said ok and moved to Mason City away from my family and friends. I really had no purpose in life and being with him gave me purpose. We were both so young. I was almost sixteen, and he was eighteen.

We had been seeing each other for a couple months, and a bunch of us kids were at a gravel pit. We were on one side of the water, and there were a couple girls on the other side laying out in swimsuits and getting some sun. So, we all dared our friend to jump in and swim across to say hi to them. So, of course, he did. About halfway across the pond, something happened, and he stopped swimming and started to go under. A couple people jumped in and tried to save him. But he fought so hard. I wasn't a good enough swimmer to even attempt to save him, and I was not healed from giving birth. I felt helpless. I had to drag one person out of the water because he was so exhausted from trying to fight him and save him. Our friend drowned, and there was nothing we could do. It was horrible. I grew up in the river and couldn't swim a lick for years. Yet this young man that was seventeen years old was swimming perfect and suddenly stopped and started fighting for his life. I remember feeling numb like it wasn't real. It was like a bad dream. The weeks that followed were so sad. But I already knew about sadness. Gosh, I wondered how much sadness can be in one person's life? Today I know that there are many people that have had more pain in life than I did. But at the time, it just didn't seem possible.

I would now start a new life. He came around in March, and on July 16th, 1971, we were married. He had a good job on the railroad, and I went to work at sixteen for the federal government for a program called Neighborhood Youth Corps. To be on this program, you had to be a teenager on your own, out of school, and you had to be counseled two hours a week. I remember my counselor like it was yesterday. He taught us kids so much. If you want a nice car or a nice television, then you may need to go out to eat or to the movies a little less. You need to figure out if it is worth that before you do it. He also told us the story about the three wealthy people that lived in the same neighborhood. One owned a garbage company, one was a lawyer, and one was a doctor. One lived in a $200,000 house, one in a $300,000 house, and one in a $500,000 house. Who owned the $500,000 house? I could not believe it could possibly be the garbage man. **But it was!** He taught me life lessons every week for two hours for two years. He did this because he cared, and his goal was to help us want a better life. I will always remember him. He truly made a difference in my life far more than he ever knew. If I could see that counselor today, I would thank him for all he taught me during that time in my life.

I worked at a center for underprivileged people. Imagine that. It was a great program and helped me in many ways. I worked forty hours a week and worked there for two years. I made $1.45 per hour, and I brought home $42.50 a week. My boss was a black woman, and she was in her early seventies. She was incredible. I have never met anyone so good, honest, kind, strict, and fair in my life. She had something like twelve kids, twenty-five grandkids, and fifteen great-grandkids. She taught me that it doesn't matter if you are tall or short, skinny, or fat, black, or white. Good is good, and bad is bad. It really is that simple. I will never forget what she taught me.

We had a food shelter and a clothing shelter. We had quilting classes, cooking classes, and a club for young boys and one for young girls. We played games with the kids and taught them to cook and sew and all kinds of activities that were fun but would maybe help them prepare for their life ahead. We had a pool table, and I would play pool with the boys for hours. They were little. Maybe eight to twelve years old. I shot a good pool game in those days. And I learned from a bunch of little kids. It really was fun. They were great kids, and most of them didn't have a very good home life. And I helped a nurse teach family planning and birth control classes to young girls. She was such a good and kind woman. And she was very soft-spoken. I thought this was a good thing to do, and I only hoped I could help enough to make a difference in their lives.

I was married for a few years, and we had a lot of fun. But, oh how I longed for a baby. So, on October 29th, 1974, I had a son. He was perfect. I was going to be a good mother and give him a better life than I had. And three years later, on November 18th, 1977, I had a daughter. She was perfect in every way. We had a perfect family. But somehow, we as a couple grew apart. We were married thirteen years, and we had moved at least fifteen times. It was tough on the kids.

I got my GED, and I always seemed to get a decent job. I worked in a foundry in Charles City, Ia., somewhere around 1978, and I made $13.56 an hour. That was a lot of money back then. But foundry work was hot and dirty and hard work. I worked right next to where they poured the iron, and I took the hot cores off the line when they came out of the oven. It was over one hundred degrees in there all the time. I would be so exhausted when I got home. We wore heavy gloves. But I would still get burns all over my arms. When I went home at night, all my skin would be black under my clothes, and we didn't wear face masks. I signed up for an apprenticeship to be an electrician and was told I was sure to get it. I was so excited. Then there was a layoff, and I was part of that. I had a few other good jobs over the next few years.

And somewhere around this time, my husband and I picked rocks out of a farmer's fields to make money. And we also did some cutting corn out of bean fields. It was hard work. But it put food on the table. I think my husband and I were married too young, and we both had our own set of issues. I do believe when you marry young, that as you finish growing and maturing, sometimes, you just grow in different directions. I had big hopes and dreams, and he did not believe in them. He used to get mad at me when I told the kids they could grow up to be whatever they wanted to be. So, in the spring of 1984, we went our separate ways. I was going to be just fine. I was going to work, raise my kids, and take care of my mom. But in October, my mom died, and my life turned upside down. I really struggled with her loss. In 1984 I got divorced, and I lost my mother. I was twenty-nine with two kids to feed and care for and no one to turn to for anything. Not one person. I remember feeling so afraid of life.

My life turned upside down.

I still made mistakes.

I had filed for a divorce in September, and my plan was to raise my children, work, and take care of my mother. In October, when my mother died, my life was a mess. I had talked to her on the phone the Sunday before she passed. I remember it like it was yesterday. She was in Northern Minnesota for the summer with her husband, and they were to come home soon. She wasn't feeling well and was kind of complaining. I told her that she had to try harder and that the good Lord can't help you if you don't help yourself. I kind of scolded her. I just wanted her to fight to get well. She had been sick for about three years. But I still hoped she would get better. After midnight on Monday night, her husband called me and said she was gone. I was in shock. I cried for days. At the funeral, my eyes were almost swollen shut. It hurt beyond imagination.

I was going to take care of her, and it would have given me a purpose along with raising my kids. Between taking care of her, raising kids, and working, I would be busy. My life would be full. And I felt bad that I had scolded her a couple days before. For the days and weeks ahead, I was not in the real world. To the point, I did not realize how much it hurt my children to lose her. I was selfish, and I was angry at God for taking her when I needed her most. I now know it was a blessing because she had suffered terrible, and the life she lived and loved was gone. She was fifty-nine years old, she was blind, and she had to walk with a walker. Her young fifty-nine -year-old mind was trapped in a very sick and tired body. My only regret of this time was not being there for my children. But there was a plan. She would not suffer anymore, and I would get stronger.

But this, too, was going to take time. It took me two years before I was able to say the word Mom without crying. I was sincerely lost for about two years. I lost her when I sincerely thought I needed her the most in my life. And I wasn't in tune with my kids during this time. My son was so close to my mom, and I wasn't aware of just how much he missed her till he started sleepwalking and crying for his grandma. It broke my heart to watch him wander around in his sleep crying for her. Oh my, it was a hard time in our lives.

I felt so alone and so afraid. I was going through

a divorce from my kids' dad, and an old high school boyfriend came around and turned our lives even more upside down for a while. It was not a good time for me or my kids. It was a mistake that I have struggled to forgive myself for and will regret forever. He showed up when I was probably the most vulnerable in my life. Unfortunately, I thought he was always my first true love, and I thought we could rekindle that. We were so different and came from very different walks of life. I really think that you can't go back to someone from long ago. It sounds easy to go back to something that is already familiar. I truly believe it rarely works. You just aren't the same people that you were. I hope my kids can forgive me for that time in our lives. He was a drug addict, and I didn't even know. He was mean to me and my kids, and we were all afraid. I made poor decisions out of loneliness and fear. This went on for several months. Then finally, I was strong enough to say I was done. And it hurt so bad I could not believe it. It truly was horrible. But my kids and I were going to be ok. This was the first **Real Regret** of my life. If given the chance, I would erase this time in our lives.

Before my mother got sick, she was an extremely

strong woman. She gave this gift to her daughters. We have all three spent most of our lives as the one that took care of everyone, the one that kept our families together, the one that made all the decisions, the breadwinner most of the time, and the one who always gave way more than they ever expected in return. And we have always been ok with this because it is who we are. It's not a bad trait. But as you get older, you do get tired of always being the strong one, the understanding one, the one who must fix everything, the one who gives and gives. All three of us did reach this age. Eventually, we all grew tired.

So, by the time I was twenty-nine, I had no parents or grandparents, I had lost a brother, and I got divorced from my kids' father.

So, began a whole new chapter of my life. Mom was gone. I worked, took care of my kids, and made even more mistakes.

In June of 1979, I went to work for a great company. I resigned from that same company April 1st, 2011. I held several positions. I started as a forklift operator and loaded and unloaded trucks in Mason City, Ia. I made $4.50 an hour. And we hand loaded a lot of boxes. I remember an older gentleman that worked there, and he and I would throw boxes all day together. They weighed about seventy-five pounds. We had to stack them by hand five high along one entire side of the trailer. Then we would load a big block of them on the other side with a clamp truck. I had long arms, and he wasn't very tall, but he was strong. We did a great job together. We loaded a lot of trucks, and we would talk and got to know all about each other's lives and families. He was a nice man.

I was not there long when I was asked to run a project to rework several hundred items that required hiring several temporary employees. At this time, my husband was not working, so he came to work there on this crew. That was not a good idea. But he asked, and I agreed. Not too long after this started, a manager came from the corporate office, and he said one of us could stay and work for the corporation, or we could both stay as temporary employees. Since I had been there for a long time and he had not, we agreed it would be best if I stayed. I was so relieved because I deserved this. I then became the warehouse supervisor. I was responsible for all freight in and out. I would get calls from corporate and handwrite all the orders, I created all the bills for freight, and I kept track of all the inventory on inventory cards. It was a matter of survival to work hard at this job. And I had no idea where it was going to take me.

It was 1986, and the company I worked for sold the plant they had been using for a distribution center. The company that purchased the plant offered me a job. And I was offered a job in Minnesota with the company I already worked for. I went to my kid's dad and asked permission to take the kids to live in Minnesota. I was terrified he would say no. What would I do? But he said yes. So as scary as it was, my kids and I moved to Minnesota and started a new life.

I was a warehouse supervisor when I moved to Minnesota. It was very hard for an already established crew to accept me (a woman) when they had always worked for two men. I went home many nights and cried my heart out. If I was the only one in the office, some of them would go all over to find one of the guys to get their next assignment. I wasn't sure I was going to make it. I was homesick, lonely, and scared to death. Then one day, it was about time to go home, and "one of the guys" made a mistake on his load, and it was in the middle of the trailer. I looked at him and told him to get off his forklift. I got on it, and I unloaded that trailer, found the mistake, and reloaded it in a matter of minutes. I earned a lot of respect that day from most of them. They finally accepted me, for the most part. It felt so good to be accepted.

I remember before I moved to Minnesota, my brother Jr. told me to move to Minnesota and meet a rich man to take care of me. I looked at him and said I could never do that. I could not marry a man that I did not love. Again, this would prove to be wrong. No matter how much money he had. Oh, and he told me, "How lucky I was." I about blew a gasket. I had been working for this company most of seven years and had only missed one and a half days that I was scheduled to work. I had bronchitis and took a half-day to go to the doctor and get some medicine. I had hardly any sleep for about three days. Then I missed one day because my daughter was sick and had a high fever, and I had to stay home with her. That was it. I couldn't miss work. I had two kids to feed. I needed this job. I worked hard, and this company was the single first thing to ever believe in me. I remember thinking that so many times. I was alone with two kids, no parents or grandparents, and I moved to Minnesota because, with this company, I could hold my head up, raise my kids, and try to give them a future. I remember thinking many times it would have been so much easier to stay in Iowa and go on welfare. It really and truly would have been so much easier. LUCKY??? I don't think so. Luck had absolutely nothing to do with it. There she was, pushing with all her might. She never gave up on me. Thank God! She had to be behind me, pushing because I was scared to death.

During the next few years, I asked Mom so many times if I was going to make it. I didn't think so sometimes. But I had my mother in me. I had determination to hold my head up and hear her say, "Lola Jean, don't you ever let anyone make you think that they are better than you." "But don't you ever think that you are better than someone else either." So, every time life tried to beat me down, I would remember that and say I can do whatever I want just as well as anyone can. We are all the same. My mom said!! I have learned over the years that she was right about most things. If everyone takes the time to think back, there is someone that said something that helped them get where they are in life today. My "someone" was "My Mother."

13

〜

It was hard on my children.

My kids and I moved into a big house at first when we moved to Minnesota. But it was just too expensive. So, we moved to an apartment. I looked at apartments that were very affordable. But they didn't have security, they didn't have secure underground parking, and  they just didn't seem safe for my kids before and after school when I wasn't there. So, we moved into a nice apartment with security and a place where I felt safe and that my children were safe. I could barely afford a two-bedroom apartment. My daughter and I shared a room, and we loved it there.

We really didn't have any furniture. We didn't have any beds, but we were going to be ok. The big house we were moving out of had beds built in the bedrooms, so we didn't have any of our own. So, someone I worked with gave me a sofa. Then, the people I worked with did something I will never forget. We all sponsored a family every year at Christmas time with what we could. The people I worked with wanted me to be that family. I was so ashamed. I didn't want to take the money. I had just too much pride. But they insisted. I cried and cried. They knew I was alone and had no one to turn to for help. And they knew I was doing the best I could. They gave me the money, and I bought a single bed for my son and a King size for my daughter and me. They were both waterbeds because they were cheap. And I bought Christmas for my children. They were so good to me and my children and I will never forget any of them for as long as I live. I can never thank them enough for what they did for me. Just when life beats you down, an angel comes along and lifts you up. They were absolutely an answer to my prayers. They had become my friends, my family, and I trusted them. How could I not trust them? They believed in me. I am pretty sure my angel sent them to me. There is no other explanation.

I worked three jobs for two years. I cleaned for someone every other Saturday in my apartment building, and I did paperwork for someone five nights a week after he was done with his route as a delivery person. Some nights he wouldn't be done till midnight. I would sit up and do the paperwork and take it to the mail slot in the apartment building before I went to bed. Then my day would start all over again at five a.m. It was hard on my kids and me to live here alone and have no one to turn to. They paid the price for having a mother that worked all the time and still barely made ends meet. We lived in that apartment for a couple years. If I hadn't had to work so much, it probably would have been better. But for the most part, we were happy there. Nice people lived there, we had good friends there, and they went to a good school. And it was a safe place for all of us. One day in the hallway, my kids introduced me to the mother of their friends. She and I were both coming home from work. Me in my jeans and her in her suit. But we became the best of friends. She was another blessing sent to me from someone. She is amazing and a good friend to this day.

The person I cleaned for was an accountant, and his wife was in a body cast. I never knew why. He was kind enough that he would do my taxes for me at a very reasonable cost. When I was in his office to pick up my taxes one day, he offered to set me up in my own business of cleaning houses or businesses. I declined. I felt secure in my job, and I told him I would never be able to pay people enough to do the job I thought they should do.

After a couple years of living in the two-bedroom apartment, I borrowed $1,500 to put a down payment on a townhouse on a personal contract for deed. We were so excited to have a bigger home of our own. But money was always tight. And I think that was part of the reason my son chose the wrong crowd to hang out with. It was an extremely tough few years with him. Sometimes I think it would have been better if we would have stayed in the apartment complex and just moved to a three-bedroom apartment. My son was angry at the world. There were empty places in his heart that I just could not fill. Lord knows I tried.

Today my son is a good man, a kind man, and I am very proud of him.

But because of all his anger, he did get most of my time when I was not working. This left my daughter kind of out there on her own. I wish I had seen that at the time. I guess there just wasn't enough of me to go around, and she really got shorted. I am sorrier than she will ever know. But she is a good and kind woman. I am very proud of the woman she has become.

Having two involved parents must make such a difference when raising children. I sure wish my kids could have had that.

My kids always got new clothes, coats, and shoes for school. They were never going to be embarrassed or ashamed of who they were, as I was. But we never really had extra money for some things that maybe their friends did. It was just how it was. Most of my clothes were from Goodwill. I worked in a warehouse, and jeans, t-shirts, sweatshirts, and coats from Goodwill worked just fine. I was ok with that. They were still better than I ever had as a kid.

In the fall of 1994, I would enter into another marriage that would eventually become the **second**

biggest regret of my life. Oh, it wasn't all bad. He was a single dad of four kids, and the three youngest got inside of my heart. My instinct to save the world took over, and I was going to make a difference in their lives. And I did. Even their mother liked me. The girls told me, as adults more than once, that I made a difference in their lives. He adored me. But he also wanted to own my soul. He hid all his jealously until after we were married. Then the possessiveness took him over. He wanted to be my whole world and feel that he was the only person in the world that gave me happiness. If I had fun with my kids or friends, he was very upset. It was so hard.

So, in 2006 we divorced. He didn't want it until he found out how much my retirement was worth. Then that was all he wanted. My retirement. So, I gave him what he wanted, and we divorced. I could have fought him, and I think I would have won. Because I contributed nothing almost the entire time we were married. I quit contributing when I figured out what kind of a person he was. My wish for him is that when he is old, he is all alone with his money. I think he remarried right away and retired on the money I worked so hard for. He should be so proud of himself. I regret marrying him so much. He was the **single biggest mistake** of my life. He changed my life forever. Unfortunately, not in a good way.

In 1995 I left warehousing and went to work at the corporate office. Essentially, I was leaving my family again. They really were my family. I was an Order Services Rep, Supervisor for the parts department, Marketing and Forecast Inventory Analyst for the commercial division, and I left after being in sales for eleven years. Most people do not like change. But I have always welcomed it. I believe I have always been curious. Some say curiosity killed the cat. But it made me want to learn. There are so many different things to do. I still say I am not sure what I want to do when I grow up. I'm not done. And to work for a company that gives you that opportunity.... WOW!! I worked hard, and they were very good to me. There were and still are so many wonderful people at this company. That is why they are as successful as they are. It really is the people you work with that make it easy to go there every day and so hard to leave.

I have always liked everyone and got along with most everybody. I spent over thirty-five years there, and I only met one person that we just didn't click. This person was incredible at their job and a very good person. I really think I tried. Maybe I tried too hard. I have decided to chock this struggle up to a generation gap. I had a boss explain this to me one time. He said: "If I throw a ball up in the air and you catch it, you will show it to everyone, share it with everyone, make sure everyone knows about it, and if it is successful, you will share all the success or even let someone else have the reward for the success." If the other person catches it, they will take it and run. It is their ball; they will nurture it, keep it to themselves and want everyone to know that they made it successful on their own." WOW!" But I am not completely convinced that both personalities are good on a team. Towards the end, I would stop some days a couple blocks before I got to work, open my car door, and throw up. I would leave work every day without returning calls to my customers, and there were just not enough hours in a day to get done. I went to the doctor to see why I was throwing up like I was, and she put me through some tests, including a stress test for my heart. The conclusion was I needed to reduce the stress in my life. So, I decided it was time to resign. This job was a high-stress job, and it just seemed like the people above me didn't care. When I handed in my letter of resignation, the manager looked right at me and said, "Yeah, your supervisor told me you were having some issues." I remember this like it was yesterday. The CEO came to see me before I left, and he said to me, "It is people like you that make this company the success it is. If you ever want to come back here, you can." Well, in time, that would prove to not be true.

I love people. All kinds of people, young, old, rich, poor, shy, outgoing, confident, not confident....... it doesn't matter....... I love people. If someone needs help, I will do whatever I can to help. If they want to help me, I will let them. If they want me to teach them what I am doing, I will. I don't even care if we work in the same department. I just don't care. Most of us have a common goal. "To feel important, to feel appreciated, to feel needed, and to be success-ful." If you make sure your people are challenged and make sure they have everything to be successful, your company will be very successful.

There are always people that just want to climb to the top, and it is their goal and focus. And some of them just do not have time to stop and help, and they will never ask for help. That is ok. They are good people. They are just busy getting where they want to go. I think they are missing out sometimes. But we need people at the top, and maybe that is what it takes to get there. But the worker bees......... Now that is where I want to be. It is where I belong.

I left this company 4/1/2011. They called it retiring because I was over fifty-five. I had a new and exciting job offer working at a Golf car dealership. The owner was going to buy a fleet, and I was going to manage renting them out and making it a profitable venture. I was both excited and scared. But with a bad spring, it fell through, and I had no job. I ended up living off my 401, which cost me most of what I had left. I tried to work at home on a website business for a while. Then I decided I was going to starve, and I really needed to work around people. I figured I have something to offer somebody. But I will never have to offer another company what I have to offer the one I had worked at for over thirty-two years.

So, I contacted a VP at the company I resigned from and said I needed to go back to work. He talked to a couple people, and I was offered a contract position in IT. And on 3/26/2012, I walked back into the company I had left almost one year ago. I was contracted for six months as a business analyst to help develop and implement a new system. Now, that is an awful long way from a forklift operator. But it really was fun. Again, the people were terrific.

I had never done anything but operations for thirty-two years. And that was exactly what I had to bring to this project. I knew the operations side of the company inside and out. When I think about it, that position was about as far from being a forklift operator as you can get. And I loved it. I enjoyed this job and had the opportunity to work with so many amazing people. The six months turned into twenty-five months, and when it ended, I had a new friend that will be my close friend for the rest of my life. She is an amazing person, and I will be forever grateful that this project brought her into my life. How amazing is that?

I had a few project managers during the twenty-five months, and each of them wanted to hire me. I was also contacted by a department manager to apply for a job he had open. I did, and he coached me to make sure I passed all the interviews. But that just wasn't in the cards. I am confident it had everything to do with a certain individual. Some people can fool many people. But we all know you can fool everyone around you, but you do have to look in the mirror at the one person you can't fool every day of your life. We all need to live with who we are. So, again, I try to be nice to others, lead a good life, and give other people the benefit of the doubt. But when I look in the mirror every day, I am ok with the person looking back at me. I admit I have made many mistakes in life, and some of them have made life harder or hurt others. But those two things were never my intentions. In some ways, I am very proud of the person looking back at me in the mirror. And I remember, "Lola Jean, don't you ever let anyone make you think that they are better than you." "But don't you ever think that you are better than someone else either." My nemesis truly thought they were better than me. This person may have even convinced me that this was true for a brief time. Oh, this person is smart enough to get what they want. To me, this person was just not a nice person. They had an influencer as well. Enough of that. It is not a good memory. One I would like to bury somewhere.

On April 30th, 2014, I had a going-away party with great people, and I left the company again. This party was packed with people that were genuinely nice people. People that enjoyed working with me. It was much nicer than the first going away. It was such a sincere and wonderful farewell, and it is a memory I will cherish forever. I could have worked happily with these people for ten more years.

The farewell in 2011 still makes me angry when I think about it. But at the same time, it was just incredibly sad.

Here I was, out of work. But I had an income. I was able to draw unemployment benefits. Now the last time I drew unemployment was maybe 1980, and I received $79 a week. This time I was getting over $500 a week, and I was able to support myself. And I traded my fairly new car in on an older car, so I did not have a car payment. It was fine. I could afford a studio apartment. I was home a couple of months when a manager I had worked for previously contacted me and said he had a job he would like me to take. It was working in inside sales for a distributor that was owned by the company I had resigned from. This manager told my family at my first retirement party in 2011 that if I had been working for him, we would never have been having that retirement party. I believe that was true. This man is just an amazing person. And if your business is failing, he could no doubt turn it around. He is tough, but he is fair. You mess up, he will chew you out and make you cry. But if you work hard and do a good job, he will reward you. I will be forever grateful.

There's that angel of mine. Oh my gosh, she has never given up on me. She has not left my side for one day since I was born. I am sure of it.

I still wonder sometimes. I ask Mom and Dad, and I ask God, "What am I supposed to do now?" Is there still a plan or a purpose for me? I assume there is. But I sure wish they would tell me what it is. I have spent my whole life thinking that there is something I am supposed to do that would sincerely make a difference in people's lives. I am just not sure what it is. But again, I like to think maybe I have made a difference in some people's lives.

So, I went to work again doing what I think I do best, taking care of customers. The first two years were fabulous. I had a fabulous team and made a good living. Life was great! Then we acquired a new territory, and it was given to me because of my expertise. It was going to be a huge learning curve for the reps and for the three hundred + customers. I was assured that I would still make the same living or better. So, that was fine. I have always accepted change and a challenge. Well, it did not exactly work out that way. At this age, it changed my life. I had a plan to retire at sixty-five. But that is not really a plan anymore. So, I will work hard and try to get back to a new plan. I do not blame anyone. I think my managers believed it when they told me my income would not change with the job change and very possibly be even better. To the contrary, it postponed my retirement for two years. It was devastating. But I still had a job, and I was surviving. And I am thankful.

The next year, 2019 was better than the previous two. And now here I am 2020, and my whole life was changed, yet again. In the fall of 2019, I asked my manager if I could move and work from home for the last two years of my career. I have wonderful friends in Minnesota, where I live. But my children all lived in different states. And I have no family in

Minnesota. I really miss my kids and grandkids. My oldest child lives in Iowa, my son in Wisconsin, and my youngest daughter lives in Arizona.

My child I gave up for adoption has three children that are all grown. My son in Wisconsin has a son that is grown with a son of his own and a daughter that is in her senior year. My youngest in Arizona has two little girls, that are four and seven. I am missing out on them growing up. And when you have little kids, it is nice to have a grandma around sometimes. So, maybe my youngest still needs me. Winter 2018/2019 was brutal. I had four to six feet of snow on my patio for months. I was so ready to be away from winter. So, I thought that Arizona would get me close to the little girls, get me out of winter, and might help me ease into retirement. With much thought, my manager finally decided yes, I could work from home for a couple of years. So, on November 24th, 2019, my son came to my home with a trailer, we loaded my trike and all my belongings, and my son and I left for Arizona. We were only a couple hours down the road, and a snowstorm hit Minnesota. So, we did get out of there just in time. Do you ever feel like someone is always looking out for you? I was going to miss the

Midwest, where I had lived for my entire life. I was leaving all that was familiar to me for over sixty-four years. It was exciting and scary for sure. But we were on our way.

We arrived in Arizona on Wednesday, November 27th, 2019. And so, I would once again start a new life. So, I moved into an apartment in a nice complex with my daughter being within walking distance. I now have a new plan to work from home till I retire. November 1st, 2021 was my new plan to retire. Oh, I will never be able to fully retire because of choices I have made. But I will retire from what I am doing and do a part-time job. I am thinking maybe I'll do something with no stress and maybe twenty hours a week.

I do have to say, I am very tired. I hope during this last chapter, I can find a life partner to retire with and just enjoy life. I sincerely want to share my life with someone. So, I will keep asking Mom, Dad, and God, is there a plan for me? Am I supposed to do something that I have not yet done? I think so, and when it is time to do it, I believe they will show me what it is. She has led me here for a reason. I am sure of it.

Kevin

14

∽

I always said good things come to those who wait.

In 2005 I had been searching for about thirteen years for my child that I gave up for adoption. I didn't want to interfere with his\her life. I just wanted to know I did the right thing and that he\she had a good life. As I said before, I called the attorney that handled the adoption when my baby was one year old from a phone booth, so no one would know I called. I asked if my baby was in a good home and everything was ok, and he assured me that it was. I had to take his word for it. But sometimes, you hear happy stories. Then you hear the nightmares where people adopt a child, then have one of their own, and mistreat the adopted one. I wasn't sure if I had a boy or girl. My mother led me to believe that I had a boy. I did not see my baby when it was born. Again, as I said before, I knew if I did, I would not be able to do what I really thought was the best thing for my child. I searched on the internet. I had search angels on the internet from all over the country that would do research for me. They would run driver's license lists for me from different states with the same birthday. And they would search websites for people searching. You would not believe the websites out there and the millions of people looking. I was registered on so many sites and received a lot of junk mail. It was un-believable. I went to the courthouse in the county where I gave birth and looked through books and books. Birth records are not recorded by date. Birth records are recorded by name, at least at the court-houses I visited. So, I had to go through thousands and look for the birth date of people born in that county dating back to the 1800s. I struck out there. And you must lie. If you say you are looking for someone that was adopted, they won't even let you look. You have to say you are doing genealogy research for your family. I finally called the hospital where my baby was born and asked for all my records from there. I did get a generic-looking birth record. So now I knew I had a girl. Anyway, like I said, I had been looking for about thirteen years. I finally decided that I would hire someone to find her. I found a private investigator in Des Moines, Ia., that told me he had never failed to find someone. The only hitch was, if he found the child, he would give this child a letter written from me and tell said child where I was. Then he would tell me he found her and had given her the letter. He would never tell me who this child was or where this child was. He mailed me the paperwork, and I filled it out and took it to the bank to be signed in front of a notary on a Friday. I was going to try to get my letter done and mail it with a check before I left for Mexico on Sunday. On Saturday morning, I was packing for Mexico, and my cell phone rang. Now, who would call my cell on a Saturday? I had a home phone. The person on the other end said, "Is this Lola?" I said, "yes, it is. Who is this?" Then they asked, "Did you give a baby up for adoption born on January 26th, 1971?" I said yes, and we both cried and cried. Good grief! To top it off, I had been sent two emails that I deleted without reading from the adoption site online. This person was home with a sick child from school and typed in adoption.com on the internet, entered their birth date, and there I was. I had been looking for thirteen years, and this person found me in about one minute. After I hung up, I called my other two kids and told them. They came right over. We shared pictures over the internet, and I got to see pictures of this child and their family. And she got to see pictures of me and her brother and sister. But I was going to Mexico in the morning. So, we had to wait a week to meet. I am pretty sure the anxiety we both went through that week was enormous. I drove to the address the following weekend, and when I pulled up in front of the house, I should have been a basket case. But I wasn't. It felt good and right because this child was ready. When I arrived, there was a photo album all made for me of the life this child had lived. And some baby clothes laid out. It was just the two of us, and we cried and hugged and talked. I heard all about the wonderful life my baby had. The parents were always honest about the adoption. But the parents made sure their child did not want for anything or miss out on life's experiences. The adoptive mother always told her child that she would help look, if-and-when their child ever wanted to search for me. When she decided to look that day, she said it was because she had such a great life and everything she could ever want, and it was a time when she had room for me.

Then she said her parents wanted to meet me. *Now I was a basket case.* So, we went to their house. The mother met me at the door and hugged me, and we both cried. She thanked me for giving her the greatest gift in the world. We shared stories, and she told me of the day that the attorney brought them their baby. She was so excited. And when their baby arrived, she said she thought the buttons would pop off the new daddy's shirt. They were both so proud. I knew from that day that I was no threat to them. They are her parents. She and her adopted mother are so close and so much alike. And the dad is just a great guy. I could not have hand-picked better parents for the baby I gave up. They are so wonderful, and this child lived a life all children should get to live. It is so much more than I ever hoped for. She has a terrific family with three beautiful children. The two youngest are twins.

In September of 2018, the child I gave up for adoption asked me to join an online family history site. So, I did. Then in February of 2019, she asked me to join yet another online family history site. So again, I did. We both started family trees, and this child found their family on their father's side that they never knew. And, of course, it led us to the birth father.

He lived in an apartment with his ninety-nine-year-old mother. He has been taking care of her for many years. I contacted him and went to see them. It was something I needed to do for me. I needed to know why he disappeared after promising me everything was going to be alright. He told me a very long story of how he went home that night and fought with his dad. He packed a duffle bag that night and left home to go live with his brother somewhere in the Carolina's, I think.

But it really didn't matter why anymore. I went to see him, and there were no butterflies, no feelings, no hope, and no reason to ever see each other again. But I could finally put that to rest in the past. I did not love him or hate him. There were no feelings at all. It was a real finalization to that time in my life. I moved on with life, and he and I are about as different as we could possibly be.

15

◦◦

It is now January of 2022. Be careful what you look for.

In February of 2019, my two nieces, Kelly and Robbyn, joined an online family history site that I already belonged to. (My sister Joyce's two daughters) In July 2019, Kelly asked me why she was related to so many people (in my dad's relatives) and my child I gave up for adoption, and I were not? I did not even think about it for one minute, and I replied, "Because my dad was probably not my dad." So be careful if you join an online family history site that you are prepared to find what you might find. I have always thought I am so different from my family. I used to tell Mom that I thought she brought the wrong baby home from the hospital. I do not look like them, and my personality has always been simply different than that of my families. I rationalized this with my age being a whole different generation than most of my brothers and sisters.

I am not sure how I feel about this. If I were younger and my mother was alive, I am sure I would have been furious. Now I wonder, why didn't Mom tell me? She had to know. Maybe that is why she seemed to treat me diffcrent than the rest of her children. Again, I assumed this was because I was the only child she had for a long time. She did not tell me about a brother she had either. I think people used to be very sure no one would ever find out these secrets. They never dreamed there would be something like the internet. And for sure, they never dreamed there would be a site that collected DNA samples and showed you your heritage and relatives.

So, I guess I feel that it is kind of like an adoptee. Imagine that!! To me, my dad was my dad, and I loved him very much. And I know he loved me as well. He used to come visit just me and bring me treats. He was my dad. This is going to tell some people that I am not their cousin or relative at all. But it really does not change how I feel about them. I love all my family. They have always been my family, and they always will be.

I did find a half-brother and sister on the online family history site. I contacted them on the site, and the girl let me know that her father died when she was little in a traffic accident. She also told me that if what I was saying was true, I was born between her and her brother. She said that would shatter the memory of her father being a perfect father. I really felt bad for her. I certainly do not want to make anyone's memory of their parent to be sad. She said we could talk sometime if I was ever in Tucson because that is where she lives. She left Iowa several years ago. I have been in Tucson for over two years now, and I have not contacted her. But I have thought about it. We will see. I never heard from her brother, who lived very close to me in Minnesota, when I contacted him. That's ok.

I will leave you with this.

I possibly have had more curves and roadblocks on this journey than many people. If I could change some things, I might. I think I would cancel the second marriage and round two of dating my childhood sweetheart. And I would have put my life on complete hold to raise my two kids and protect them from harm. But we cannot move forward wishing we could change the past. This journey has made me who I am. And for the most part, I am ok with who I am. I have made many mistakes. And I must live with those to the best of my ability. But we all do.

A special thank you to My Family and to My Angel for never giving up on me.
"Some of My Life Lessons"

- In business, you are only as good as the people that work for you. Earn their respect and empower them to do great things. Together you can move mountains. Honestly, it is true. I have seen it with my own eyes.
- If I ever worked in a woman's shelter, I would tell them that it is at least one hundred times harder to do it on your own than it is to go back to abuse. BUT!!! You can. You really can. And when you do, it is like winning the lottery. You feel good about yourself. You can

hold your head up. I do not think anyone tells them they can do it. It really does get easier.

- Tell young people they are the new foundation that will literally build the world their children will live in. Keep telling them how terrific they are till they believe they can do anything. Because they can.
- Treat the world like it is a beautiful house. If you really look at it, it is unbelievably beautiful. Too many people are moving too fast to stop and look.
- Did you know if you smile at people, they almost always smile back? Even if they are crabby. I am sure I have annoyed people. Oh, well. ☺ Try it. This starts when we are babies. If someone is having a bad day, you can make their life a little better and not say a word.
- If you do not know where or what you want to be, find a company like I did that has endless opportunities for someone that wants to work hard. It is getting tougher. But I can only hope there are still companies like this. Do not be afraid. Try new things.
- I have lived in a house full of people and been lonely. Loneliness is a horrible feeling.

- A woman told me once that the reason I want to save the world is because no one saved me. Now that is something to think about. Wow!! But I believe I was saved. I have had a full life with many good things in it. She was saved too. She has just never realized it.

- I really do wish I could save the world and make everyone see what it is they have right in front of them. Silly huh?

- If you hold your children close, it should always make them feel safe and loved. It should never be an unpleasant experience. They trust you.

- Tell your children that hugs are the only vitamin that everyone must have every day, forever and ever. Hugs are amazing. It's human touch, and it is true.

- This one makes me crazy. I have seen so many women that are threatened by their mother–in–law. She is your husband's mother. He will never love you as much as he loves her. But he will never love her as much as he loves you either. It is two very distinct kinds of love. Think about it. You cannot compete. There is no competition to take part in. Good grief. If he respects or worships his mother, then he will treat you the same. Feel lucky that she did a good job. Even thank her some time. Why don't some people get it? I had a woman tell me one time that every time they go to her husband's mother's house, she fusses over him, makes all his favorite food, and is somewhat ridiculous. She lets her. It gives her some joy, and the daughter-in-law can go read a book. The day you become a mother, someone needs you, and you really do not ever want that to stop. Everyone needs to feel needed sometimes. And you hope your children always need you. And it is ok. It doesn't hurt anyone. I wish I had figured this out when I was much younger. I have seen too many women miss out on a great relationship with a fantastic lady because of this.

- There are parts of my childhood I wish all kids could experience. We rode our bikes, swam in the river, and walked all over town. And we never worried about being taken or hurt. And I truly do have some great memories.

- The most important lesson of all in this life

is: Protect your children from harm when they are small. It will make it easier for you to grow old. I failed this one. And because of that, I will grow old with almost unbearable pain in my heart.

- I wish someone would have explained to me how to teach my children. I was too busy working all the time. I wish I would have let them be my purpose and the only purpose I needed. This I did not know. I didn't let them fill my loneliness, and I didn't fill theirs. And I did not know this then. I don't believe I had a teacher. So, for me, it was trial and error. It is hard when you are alone. I made so many mistakes, and I wish I could stop all future parents from making those mistakes. It would possibly save them from crying a million tears or more someday. I have cried many more.

- I always said my mother lied to me about one thing in life. It was not really a lie. But she raised me to think that the way it is supposed to be is, "You grow up, get married, have babies, and your husband should take care of you." Oh my, my life could not have been farther from the truth. I have never been taken care of. At this point, I doubt that is ever going to happen.

- Mom used to say, "It takes all kinds of people to make the world go around" "It would be boring if we were all the same." YUP! She was right again. I believe that women knew everything. Just a small-town Mom with no education. Imagine that. I find her to be more amazing all the time, and she has been gone for over thirty years. If I had only known all of this before she left this earth to be with her maker.

- I still miss her terribly every day. I still tell her what an amazing woman she was **to me** in so many ways. And I miss my dad so much. I have learned more about him the last ten years simply because I have asked many questions. He has been gone over fifty-eight years. I ask Mom, and I ask Dad to watch over my children and their families. I still ask their advice and can only hope I have made Mom and Dad both proud of me.

- But most important, "I am proud of me," "I struggled in life and prevailed" Remember,

"It's not a miracle" Everyone can get through their hardships in life. You just must remember, "you can do anything as well as anyone else if that is what you truly desire."

• We are all God's children. If you just believe, your guardian angel will lead you to Him. Some of us take longer to realize we have someone watching over us. I think I always knew, but I just didn't understand. So, I led my angel down the longest road there was. But no matter the time and distance, my angel never gave up on me. She has been my guardian, my teacher, and always believed in me even when I maybe didn't believe in myself. I am learning more every day to let my life be full by having faith. Believe me, I have a long way to go. But I am getting there.

I believe God leaves the door open if He knows you are on your way.
God Bless you all, Lola.

Lola Hewitt grew up in Nora Springs, Iowa. A small town with a population of 1337.
She moved to the twin cities in 1984, spent most of 42 years taking care of customers for one company, and found it very rewarding.
Lola's experiences in life are what she enjoys writing about most.
Aside from writing and spending time with family and friends, she enjoys the outdoors, golf, riding motorcycles, baking, and DIY projects.